CENTAURS, RIOTING IN THESSALY

Martyn Hudson

Centaurs, rioting in Thessaly

punctum books

CENTAURS, RIOTING IN THESSALY
© 2017 Martyn Hudson

http://creativecommons.org/licenses/by-nc-sa/4.0/

This work carries a Creative Commons BY-NC-SA 4.0 International license, which means that you are free to copy and redistribute the material in any medium or format, and you may also remix, transform and build upon the material, as long as you clearly attribute the work to the authors (but not in a way that suggests the authors or punctum endorses you and your work), you do not use this work for commercial gain in any form whatsoever, and that for any remixing and transformation, you distribute your rebuild under the same license.

First published in 2017 by
punctum books
Earth, Milky Way
punctumbooks.com

punctum books is an independent, open-access publisher dedicated to radically creative modes of intellectual inquiry and writing across a whimsical para-humanities assemblage. We solicit and pimp quixotic, sagely mad engagements with textual thought-bodies. We provide shelters for intellectual vagabonds.

ISBN-13: 978-1-947447-40-0 (print)
ISBN-13: 978-1-947447-41-7 (ePDF)
LCCN: 2017962641.

Cover image: Bobby Benjamin and Hannah Pedersen.
Design: Chris Piuma.
Editorial assistance: Shant Rising & Vincent van Gerven Oei.

Table of contents

A note on the text, viii.
Acknowledgments, ix.
Introduction: Centaurs, rioting at Thessaly, xi.

1. Never never lands, 1.
2. Looking for centaurs, 15.
3. Surveying the labyrinth, 35.
4. Daedalus and his machines, 47.
5. Ghosts, reading, and repetition, 67.

Conclusion: Centaurs, human and non-human, 93.

A note on the text

For a text that is largely about the recurrence of visual motifs, it might seem ironic that there are no pictures. Part of the process of reading the text is the summoning up of those ghosts/revenants by the readers themselves. I note in the text that this is not a work of classical studies and it does not seek to understand the origin, context, and detail of aspects of the classical world except in their resonance outside of their original emergence. There are also geographical dislocations, most significantly between the city-states of the Hellenic mainland and the Ionian islands, so even though the Centaur myths were most associated with Thessaly, some commentators see the emergence of central aspects of the classical world not in Sparta or Athens but in the island states of Ionia. If philosophical and political thought today at least owes something to Ionia, then this may be because of its location and its fracture and hybris amongst emerging, competing, and complex civilisations and cultures. Central aspects of the classical world survived only in non-European civilisations and that world and its legacies were constructed in complex interrelationships with many other civilisational forces.

Acknowledgments

I would like to acknowledge the following in the development of the ideas in this book; Ruth Barker, Harriet Manning, Trevor Hussey, Paul Watt, Kevin Stenson, John Bowers, Eric Cross, Ben Jones, Ben Freeth, David Ames Curtis, Carl Dunn, Mark Richards, Marie-Lan Nguyen, Neil Jenkings, Tom Schofield, Julie Crawshaw, Frances Rowe, Richard Skelton, Stephen Speed, Colin Tipton, Keith Macdonald, Eileen Joy, Amelia Knowlson, Liv Carder.

This book is dedicated to Phil Balmforth, my first teacher of classics.

introduction

Centaurs, rioting in Thessaly

> I cannot ignore the fact that my own thought, however original I may deem it to be, is but a ripple, at best a wave, in the huge social-historical stream which welled up in Ionia twenty-five centuries ago.
> —Cornelius Castoriadis[1]

Much of the thought and the practice of human life is irredeemably related to Ionia, to Achaea, to classical Greek civilisation. Certainly one, if not the only one, of the central imaginings of ourselves and our world is Ionian. Our mapping of ourselves in our world also owes a huge debt to the classical. The emergence, materialisation, and extra-territorialisation of Ionian spaces of philosophy and democracy indelibly mark our world. The very concept of the *human* is Ionian even if comparable ideas of the human emerge in the world of Genesis and Gilgamesh. But here darkness emerges just as the human Achaeans emerged from darkness into history. Ionian spaces are also spaces where there are indecisions about whether our being is human or animal, where there are fractures between civilisations resting

---

1 Cornelius Castoriadis, *Philosophy, Politics, Autonomy: Essays in Political Philosophy* (Oxford: Oxford University Press, 1991), 19.

upon categories of barbarism,[2] and where exist the horrors of the Ionian spaces as slave states.[3] The Persian expedition of Xenophon was a journey across territory and into battle, but it was also a journey into human separation and a reflection on human darkness. We are but footnotes of Ionian history and philosophy — we replicate time and time again the darkness and the light. The question of the barbarian is central to classical thought in terms of self-definition. Often the confusions about the human have their origins in a process of demarcation between peoples — specifically around the seams and borders between them. But peoples in movement are syncretic even if their hybridities are confusing and often irrational.

The porous, permeable boundaries (even if we could detect those borders) of the human are time and time again challenged by the way we imagine ourselves and others. That humanness, through our capacity to plan and design and imagine, is extended into our buildings and machines and our art. Ionians dissolved and re-imagined their being constantly through playing with the ideas of barbarian and animal — and specifically the imagining of Centaurs and other hybrid species. Ionians imagined and designed labyrinths to both lose and find themselves and others. They fought and eventually conquered the city of Troy — perhaps the origin of some of world history's most potent, if mundane, labyrinth myths.[4] The Ionians created toys and machines for themselves which enhanced the very idea

---

2   See Edith Hall, *Inventing the Barbarian: Greek Self-Definition through Tragedy* (Oxford: Clarendon, 1989), 1–2, for the beginning of an analysis of Greek ethnic *self-consciousness* through the development of tragedy.
3   See Naoise Mac Sweeney, *Foundation Myths and Politics in Ancient Ionia* (Cambridge: Cambridge University Press, 2013).
4   Oliver Taplin, *Homeric Soundings: The Shaping of the Iliad* (Oxford: Oxford University Press, 1992).

of the human and extended it into the realms of birds and gods. Their prosthetic wings allowed them to escape the labyrinth and fly into the sky. This may have been myth, but what is myth but the lived reality of imagination, the stories we tell ourselves about us and what we are?[5]

Those stories come to us as repetitions and to be repeated again. They often come from the libraries and the documentation of other civilisations after the collapse and disintegration of the classical world. They are sometimes encoded in the artefacts that are the remnants of Ionian civilisation. The actual origins and meaning of those stories and imaginings are often lost to us but it doesn't stop us replicating them for our own purposes. The constant proliferation of labyrinths in our art and in our fields and the reworking and re-display of Centaurs in our museums and books display an obsession with a set of repetitive motifs. Centaurs, labyrinths, the Icarus legend are just three amongst many others; Circe, the Atreides, Oedipus, Antigone, Calypso, Clytemnestra, the Maenads, Achilles, Helen and Paris, the wooden horse, Hades.[6] Greek dramatic theatre displays them all time and time again.[7] Some of the most powerful myths that we repeat today are but footnotes or marginalia in other stories. The capacity to revivify a motif is often grounded on its discovery or its perpetuation into any given historical moment. Often they are recompositions of multiply transferred stories as in the use of the classical by

---

5 For a general introduction to the 'thought worlds' of classical civilisation, see Anthony Andrewes, *Greek Society* (Harmondsworth: Penguin, 1991) and H.D.F. Kitto, *The Greeks* (Harmondsworth: Penguin, 1957).
6 R.G. Austin, 'Virgil and the Wooden Horse', *Journal of Roman Studies* 49 (1959): 16–25.
7 See Rush Rehm, *Radical Theatre: Greek Tragedy and the Modern World* (London: Duckworth, 2003), and *Greek Tragic Theatre* (London: Routledge, 1992).

English dramatists. Perhaps more mysteriously, the constant perpetuation and rebuilding of labyrinths indicate their utility for ways of thinking about ourselves as if their building and their traverse could solve something for us, now, rather than hint at some opaque and inaccessible origin.

This book is not about any kind of understanding of classical Greek civilisation — it is not a work within the corpus of *classics*. It is the work of a reader entranced by some mythic motifs that recur in his life time and time again. This book is about humans and their obsession with understanding themselves through repetition — specifically a set of motifs that emerge from classical Ionia. It is about reading and about how reading books and images almost compel us to repeat their stories and themes as if they were fairytales.[8] The almost constant production and reproduction of motifs of Centaurs, labyrinths, and flying human beings is how we come to understand ourselves now as human beings, just as others before us in Ionia were obsessed with the same process. Understanding the origin of these motifs is part of classical studies, as is the decipherment of languages, and the mapping of the ancient world. Our book is not about those original beings that ran across the mountains of Thessaly but about the effects that they have had upon us in the present and their social power.

Fairytales happen in lands, more precisely the land above and the land below. Often humans were held captive in fairyland, taken from the realm of the sun into that of darkness. We are deluding ourselves if we think that Faerie is more imaginary than the world in which those humans walked. We walk, above and below, amongst magical precipices. Our world is

---

8 Graham Anderson, *Fairytale in the Ancient World* (London and New York: Routledge, 2000).

enmeshed with fabrication and fiction and is not the less real for that. Accounts of traversing Faerie or the world of the dead, of seeing gods and Centaurs, abound. They might even be delusions, but they delineate something profound about our capacity to imagine lands and worlds. For many of us Narnia and its maps are a more significant presence than the world beyond our door. So, the space of Ionia is an imaginary space. Centaurs riot in the Thessaly of our imagination, Troy is broken up still in our stories, and the Achaeans traverse the steps towards its centre. It would be unforgiveable if historical practice forgot this — that the story-worlds of our ancestors and ourselves are as real to us as the artefacts which we make out of them and which still survive, even if in fragments like our stories.

In the first chapter we examine the territory of classical discourse, perhaps as we enter the camp of the Achaeans upon the plains of Troy. This is a camp, however, of our own making. Troy remains a cipher and a metaphor — even if the meanings it carries and delivers to us are obtuse and opaque. These are what Moses Finley in his critical theory of the classical world has called the 'Never Never lands'[9] of Ionia — fabrications, fictions, imaginaries whose ultimate and original meaning is lost to us and can never be recovered. The idea of the Never land was developed by Finley to denote the world of Odysseus and his adventures and to question the ways in which some used the Homeric text to locate real places and destinations. The relation of the text to the world and the world to the text is fluid — we read through the text to the world just as we situate their texts within contexts of worlds. But our Never land is the imaginary space from which subsequent peoples, including

---

9   M.I. Finley, *The World of Odysseus* (London: Pimlico, 1999), 51.

archaeologists like Schliemann, have extracted their motifs and treasures.

In the second chapter we look at the recurring figure of the Centaur and why it casts its shadow so obsessively across our history. If the Centaur, as it takes a pause from battling its Lapith enemies, can be tracked across the plains of Thessaly, what might this mean for both historical method and its search to reveal antiquity and at the same time illustrate something about why it recurs in human narrative and art so frequently? The Centaur is a cipher. It can represent Barbary, or the human relation to animals, or Persians, or many other things. The Centauromachy and its origin is literally enshrouded in myth and one hopes that new ways that historians might approach the classical world might reveal more about its emergence. Meanwhile, we continue to repeat it, to replicate it, to recompose it because it does something for us. We use it as essentially an artefact to think with. At the same time we still have unrevealed the reason why it is so ubiquitous from classical aesthetics onwards and why its repetition is so compelling.

In the third chapter we look at another motif of repetition — that of the labyrinth. Children still frequent the byways of labyrinths. They are still a central theme of our literature, a central metaphor for our world and why we are lost in it. But like the Never lands of Ionia it is a fiction, fabrication, and imaginary — yet one which is built and rebuilt constantly in human cultures. Some have considered the centre of the labyrinth as the entrance to underworlds, its traverse as a walk to the land of the dead. Others have seen the labyrinth as a literal or metaphorical mapping of the route towards monsters either internal or external to us. It occurs in different forms across many civilisations, even in archaic games scratched in walls by ancient labourers. The classical version is at times located within discourses of monsters, sometimes Centaurs but more often that other hybrid, syncretic beast — the Minotaur. This classical version has even, by some, been located in the specific material spaces of the palace of Knossos. The proliferation and elaboration of the myth of Theseus and Ariadne is located at least in the fabricated version of that labyrinth. It is still with us and we still rework and build those labyrinths. Perhaps significantly the ancients locate the work of building the labyrinth in the design and labour of a human being. Not only does this say something to us about the fabrication of our material world, it also suggests perhaps that we can measure it, understand it, map and survey it. If we cannot survey the products of our being then we will be even less able to survey the worlds and doings of gods.

In the fourth chapter we examine the maker, engineer, designer of the labyrinth. Not only is Daedalus a craftsperson but he is obsessed with the boundaries of buildings and worlds and the borders to be transgressed between the human and the non-human. His attempts to create animal-hybrid engines of movement, much like the hybrid beings of the Centaurs tell us something about both humanness and the act of creation.

In the final chapter we conclude by trying to understand why Ionian spaces and imaginaries are so important for our current projects to ask humanity to change itself. Not to reform or revolutionise human nature, but ask it to think again and again about its different manifestations. The return to the ghosts of the Achaean camp can illustrate our social and political practice in the world we fabricate and make for ourselves, as we newly fabricate and extend our own bodies with machines. Repetition and recomposition achieve their social power in the inhabitation of ghosts within real and active human frames and social relations. The dead of world history emerge time and time again.

chapter one

Never never lands

> I am not certain that we have registered an appropriate astonishment, even, perhaps, a condign sense of scandal, at the persistently repetitive and 'epigonal' tenor of so much of our consciousness and expressive forms. Did the nerve of symbolic invention, of compelling metaphor, die with Athens?
> —George Steiner[1]

Ionia has disappeared, Troy is no more, Antigone and the heroes are gone. But then, they were never there in the first place. Scholars have used the poetry of Homer and the tragedies of Aeschylus as texts full of clues to try and understand the societies which produced them. Other scholars, more intent upon the aesthetics of the text, have looked to the world surrounding them to illustrate problems within the text. No matter — the *classics* are not our concern. It is the shadows and ghosts of Ionia, Troy and the heroes, with which we are concerned not their original locations or their lost human frames. Thessaly is an imaginary space. There is no intention here to repeat or reconstruct — only to understand the ubiquity of those repetitions and reconstructions. Those repetitions are quite literally

---

1 George Steiner, *Antigones: The Antigone Myth in Western Literature, Art and Thought* (Oxford: Oxford University Press, 1986), 122–23.

astonishing. It is almost as if, as George Steiner says, our nerve of invention was just born and then died in the *city-state* of Athens. Cities are rebuilt, heroes are made to stalk the land again, the dead rise once more from their graves. Indeed, there are other sources of imagination and invention beyond Ionia in the desert tribes of Canaan, in Egypt, and elsewhere. The compulsion to *re-form* and repeat, to understand ourselves as the products of dead generations is everywhere.[2] The ghosts of the Oresteia haunt our imaginations as Agamemnon treads upon the blood red fabric.[3] The fact of so many Antigones in cultural works as well as in real historical situations alerts us to the very real presence of the past in the present before we even get to the notion of how we begin to conceive of oneself or others as an Antigone, or whether similar situations are more receptive to certain kinds of motifs. Steiner has noted that Charlotte Corday, the assassin of Marat, was seen as an Antigone by contemporaries.[4] Even a brief examination of such a process would imply that similar historical conditions create similar personages and hence analogies but in this case the analogy would soon break down outside of the imagination of Girondin Ideologues. The original Antigone, as upholder of a natural justice in the face of

---

2   Martyn Hudson, 'The Clerk of the Forester's Records: John Berger, the Dead, and the Writing of History', in *Rethinking History* 4, no. 3 (2000): 261–79, and Martyn Hudson 'On the Dead of World History', *Race and Class* 43, no. 4 (2002): 26–33.

3   Robert Fagles and W.B. Stanford, 'A Reading of 'The Oresteia': The Serpent and the Eagle', in Robert Fagles, ed., *Aeschylus: The Oresteia* (Harmondsworth: Penguin, 1997), 13–97, and see also the performances directed at The National Theatre in 1999 by Katie Mitchell, using the text and translation, Aeschylus, *The Oresteia,* trans. Ted Hughes (London: Faber, 1999).

4   Steiner, *Antigones*, 10.

Creon's statesmanship was not really an archetypal gesture to be easily incorporated into any idea of political assassination.

The destruction and dissolution of the Ionian city-states, the dispersal of their mythologies, and the collapse of their aesthetic productions would ironically lead to the perpetuation of those mythologies and political practices as they were recomposed in new civilisational moments such as the Renaissance.[5] As Judith Barringer has noted—'…the past endured—in literature, in monuments and ruins, and in memory—to be rediscovered, revered, and reviled, again and again'.[6] The city of 'Troy' was rediscovered underneath the multiple strata of history, Plato was revered in medieval Oxford, the vituperative scorn inflicted upon the 'Hun' enemy in the First World War reminiscent of Xenophon's injunctions against Persian barbarism. England's Greece to the American Rome. The multiple reworkings of identity, architecture and philosophy was almost an exercise in compulsion—that human beings almost by reflex re-invented Ionia and the classical for their own ends. We see also the origins of totalitarianism in the city state of Sparta. As Roberto Calasso has said— 'Sparta is surrounded by the erotic aura of the boarding school, the garrison, the gymnasium, the jail. Everywhere there are *Mädchen in Uniform*, even if that uniform is a taut and glistening skin'.[7]

These compelling metaphors however carried over little actual, original meaning—even as scholars sought for clues within them. They were largely re-invented for pragmatic

---

5 Luba Freedman, *The Revival of the Olympian Gods in Renaissance Art* (New York: Cambridge University Press, 2003).

6 Judith M. Barringer, *The Art and Archaeology of Ancient Greece* (Cambridge: Cambridge University Press, 2014), 407.

7 Roberto Calasso, *The Marriage of Cadmus and Harmony*, trans. Tim Parks (New York: Alfred A. Knopf, 1993), 251.

reasons not because they could actually conjure up the ideas and practices of Athenian groves. They were useful to the peoples conjuring them up. *This* was the meaning of the Circe myth, *this* is who the Cyclops was, *these* peoples are the origin of the Centaur motif. Nobody really got much further than supposition. *This* is where Agamemnon slept, *here* is where Achilles fell or Odysseus made shore. The river *Meander* in classical Turkey itself becomes a motif for art, for thought, and for understanding rivers, that is recomposed time and time again. In a sense this book follows the circuitous, circular, twisting and turning journeys of peoples, ideas, and thoughts. But is not a journey towards origins and meaning but rather away from them — towards what they bring to birth in future generations. These motifs, stories, characters are not material entities that then re-appear in some ethereal, ghostly fashion to haunt our imaginations. They are phantasms to begin with which then become materialised, quite literally, in our cultures. The Never lands of the classical furnish our museums, boulevards, homes and literatures. The Furietti Centaurs are material entities recomposed from ethereal and fragmented stories. As Steiner says 'It is a defining trait of western culture after Jerusalem and after Athens that in it men and women re-enact, more or less consciously, the major gestures, the exemplary symbolic motions, set before them by antique imaginings and formulations'.[8]

This is not to say that fiction and fabrication are not part of real material processes but like anything material practices of art, building, human life are essentially imaginary. If 'The Greeks provided the chromosomes of Western civilization'[9] and they

---

8   Steiner, *Antigones*, 108.
9   Charles Freeman, *The Greek Achievement: The Foundation of the Western World* (Harmondsworth: Allen Lane, 1999), 434.

might have done so, in part, quite literally, they also provided imaginary ancestries, lineages and genealogies from the mythological connection between the first Kings of Britain and Rome as part of the Trojan diaspora conquered by the Achaeans to our practice of mathematics and logic. This is not to deny the part of the monotheistic religions of Judaism, Islam and Christianity as having their own modes of repetition and compulsion, just that they themselves often find recourse to the judgement of classical ancestors such as Alexander the Great in Islam. This is the productive logic of imagination that the classical becomes the matrix for understanding our bearing and being as a human species.

In his discussion of the production throughout history of the multiple *Antigones* George Steiner has argued for the continued imaginative presence of dead and ghostly beings and entities. For Steiner 'The Minotaur inhabits our labyrinths and our flyers plummet from the sky like Icarus'.[10] How to hold ourselves, to articulate, to gesture — these can be products just as much of the classical than our mothers and fathers. Our vocabularies and methods of understanding are quite literally archaic, if recomposed. For Steiner and the Greeks — 'It is by their light that we set out. It is they who first set down the similes, the metaphors, the lineaments of accord and of negation, by which we organize our inward lives'.[11] Crucially, the organisation of the inward life is an organisation born of permeability, porousness, confusion about who we are and how to classify ourselves and the things around us. Metaphors are produced as an attempt to make sense of what we are as human beings. Classical adventures are 'forays into the border countries of chaos'

---

10 Steiner, *Antigones*, 129.
11 Steiner, *Antigones*, 133.

where hybrid species meet each other, in contest and battle, to create classification systems of what is human and what is not.[12] The 'border countries of chaos' are the lands of Ionia — the liminality of the human its central problematic. No wonder that those metaphors in such distant locations and times as ours continue to be so compelling. Demarcation, expulsion, identification are as much a part of our inward lives as ever.

The Ionians were a composite set of peoples, biological and cultural hybrids.[13] Further, their being, argues Moses Finley, refuted the idea of an 'integrated psychic whole'. They were ultimately fluid, human identities.[14] The permeability of those identities was about peoples and cultures, but also about humans, animals and objects. What it meant to be human was generous and expansive. But the human was also intimately related to the divine and the almost human gods of the classical world. As Moses Finley notes,

> The humanization of the gods was a step of astonishing boldness. To picture supernatural beings not as vague, formless spirits, or as monstrous shapes, half bird, half animal, for instance, but as men and women, with human organs and human passions demanded the greatest audacity and pride in one's own humanity.[15]

The idea that gods and magical beings could walk the same earth as humans and intervene in their world says much about the mythological reality and imaginary of that world. These entities

---

12 Steiner, *Antigones*, 136.
13 M.I. Finley, *The World of Odysseus* (London: Pimlico, 1999), 17.
14 Finley, *Odysseus*, 25.
15 Finley, *Odysseus*, 135.

were literally of flesh and blood and walked about as humans did. How easy it was though in ancient stories for humans to emerge out of dust, or to be turned into stone. The border lines between stones and humans and wolves and humans were contested. Little wonder that renaissance art would produce other versions of these beings in stone — replica's of prior entities, as human and as equine as any woman or horse we might see today, but combined into a new confederation of being. The dissolution of those borders was also about the dissolution of the boundaries between soul and soul. The soul would flee from being into being or leave its material human frame in the world above in order to enter the world below. Often that route was a physical traverse across a 'real territory'. Hades had a material entrance, Zeus was born beneath a real mountain. This did not make these metamorphoses less imaginary.

But the perpetuation of metaphor into our own world is also rooted in the fact that our classical inheritance is not one of totality or comprehensiveness. In fact, the inheritance (often through survival in the great libraries of Islam) is one of fragments and general incomprehensibility with flashes of recognition. Only a few remnants survive of Greek tragic drama, only two out of the many books of Homer. We have chosen the guiding metaphors of our civilisation out of wreckage and disaster. The artefacts we have been able to glean we have used. Others were consigned to the darkness. But this also gives rise to an intriguing question — were the stories of gods walking among humans themselves fictions or were they the half-remembered realities of an archaic past — distorted memories of real events like the Trojan war itself? No matter, their shadows and effects are the same and we shall never know those origins except through supposition.

Ionia is what Moses Finley has called the 'Never Never Land' of classical antiquity. The world of Odysseus never quite existed.[16] Just as the Centaurs and the Cyclops never quite existed. That does not mean that they are not 'existents' as, like gods and angels, they are real presences to whole peoples and cultures and continue to exist in our civilisations as remnants of those past worlds. But of course, even if half-remembered, they are also symbolic entities expressing abstract ideas in human and non-human form specifically about what humans are and how they shade into other beings. Perhaps ironically if we can continue to use the idea of 'half-remembrance' — which half of the Centaur is the 'remembered reality' when each half is explicitly taken from 'real' humans and horses and combined into this new hybrid entity which no-one 'actually' saw? If, as both Finley and Steiner maintain, the classical Greeks were obsessed with actuality and the concrete and invested all of their most abstract symbolic and spiritual ideas in the form of real entities, what are the Greeks actually 'seeing' when they depict the Centaur? Even if, as Steiner notes, the imaginary entities were of bone and marrow.[17] This isn't the space to rehearse the complex analytics of what the gods and heroes embodied in their frames; abstract ideas of justice, the idea of will, the notion of weather or message or love, or the hunt. Nor what supposedly real human beings represented in these stories like Daedalus and his making.

The constant imaginary reproduction and recomposition of visual 'existents' is complicated, as we have seen, by the fact that their originals are no longer or never were existent. They are not visual representations of originary artefacts but creations

---

16 Finley, *Odysseus*, 51, 101.
17 Steiner, *Antigones*, 44.

across space and time and enmeshed in a complex series of social practices, contestations and functions.[18] They are material presences standing in the place of absences. They bring into question the ontology of the human. The structural, spatial labyrinth, the biological entity of the Centaur built by words and images, the designer of the labyrinth Daedalus, each displays a different facet of recomposition. Fundamentally these are about recompositions of the idea of the human and what it can become by design. But they are also about the terror and the horror felt by humans towards non-humans and specifically the fear that their very humanness would be recomposed by metamorphosis into another being, or even worse a hybrid conjunction with another being. Ovid's *Metamorphoses* begins with one transformation and this does not end until the closure of the work.[19] This fear of instability, of the dialectic, is a fear that as one changes some essential part of oneself is transferred into the new being — elevated, preserved, whilst other parts are relegated or cancelled.

Daedalus solves this problem of metamorphosis by attaching wings as *tools* not as conjunctions and combinations of the essential being of human and bird. The Never land is a place where beings are combined and contested but also places which are built and traversed and where things are made. In the classical world the contestation was often between beings that

---

18 As Marx and Engels make clear — 'If in all ideology man and their circumstances appear upside-down as in a camera obscura, this phenomenon arises just as much from their historical life-process as the inversion of objects on the retina does from their physical life-process,' Karl Marx and Friedrich Engels, *The German Ideology, Part One* (London: Lawrence and Wishart, 1970), 47.

19 Warren Ginsberg, 'Ovid's "Metamorphoses" and the Politics of Interpretation', *The Classical Journal* 84, no. 3 (1989): 222–31.

were made and those that made themselves. Humans had the power to look at the syncretic and make themselves time and time again in a circular rotation of observation and replication. Unlucky and unhappy Gregor Samsa, in Kafka's *Metamorphosis*, who woke up and simply found himself transformed with his own being and will locked inside a terrifying monster that he could not operate effectively — made rather than making.

These three motifs, that of the Labyrinth, of the Centaur, and of Daedalus, delineate separate aspects of that social life — how to describe the world and what it is and how to describe the human and what it is. The fact that these are specifically visual manifestation of the imaginary of the social-historical is significant in the sense that they are the recurring echoes of something that once-existed or never-existed. Yet the fact that they recur time and time again in human history testifies to a function that they might perform. Understanding these motifs means we have to navigate a series of problems; how to describe a visual artefact and the methods we would need to do that, how we can assess the provenance of an artefact and examine its production out of complex sets of social and historical relations, and how we can discern the manner in which artefacts themselves have social powers to produce and structure social relations. Examining the social production of an artefact and its social constitution means describing the kinds of social relations that are invested in it and methodically describing its 'meaning' by which we mean the kinds of things that the visual artefact represents.

Often in this sense describing the artefact itself means the mapping of what it represents and what social powers it might have. We can think of these visual artefacts and our ways of seeing them as social and historically constituted. But what is the status of visual artefacts that exist now but which represent 'non-existents', 'once-existent but no more', or 'phantasmic existents' — in the latter case those things that are purely the invention of the imagination? Further, what is offered in the examination of these artefacts and visual entities or what Heidegger has called the 'Seiendes' — the entity that 'is'? Are they historical objects and what do they disclose if interrogated? Further, like Heidegger's 'productive logic' do these entities have some kind of 'reproductive logic' across space and time?[20] Heidegger, himself obsessed with the classical world, was concerned with this question of being as 'what is' and noted the incapacity of philosophy to begin to address this question. He argued that the concept of 'being' had been relegated in Greek philosophy as a theme for 'actual investigation', an investigation which had only been 'fragmentary and incipient'.[21] Heidegger's concern is inquiry; what do we ask of an object, what do we interrogate? Further, what do entities disclose to us and articulate in their being?[22]

If seeing is 'social' and not a delusion[23], and if what we see represents or embodies something important for that social formation, what possible 'meaning' or 'message' can the visual existents of Centaurs and labyrinths hold stable in different social and historical locations? If our human nature is fundamentally socially produced then that nature and the themes it

---

20 Martin Heidegger, *Being and Time/Sein und Zeit*, trans. John Macquarrie and Edward Robinson (Oxford: Basil Blackwell, 1962), 22, 30.
21 Heidegger, *Being and Time*, 21. See also the 'tool-analysis' and the concept of *Zuhandenheit* in Graham Harman, 'Technology, objects and things in Heidegger', *Cambridge Journal of Economics* 34 (2010): 17–25, 17–18.
22 Heidegger, *Being and Time*, 24–27.
23 Douglas Harper, *Visual Sociology* (London: Routledge, 2012) and Elizabeth Chaplin, *Sociology and Visual Representation* (London: Routledge, 1994).

uses to illustrate and elaborate itself are also subject to change as societies change. Why then are we so utterly compelled to reproduce the same metaphors, albeit with different codes and signs embodied within them? And why is their study so compelling for ongoing generations of scholars?[24]

The repetition and recomposition of social forms and motifs is central to social life and culture.[25] The specific visual repetition of classical forms is very much a feature of politics, aesthetics and philosophy from drama to sculpture and to the visual display of democratic power in architecture.[26] Visual presentation has long been concerned with the idea of assemblage and re-assemblage and new circulations of motifs, experiences, and forms. The visual recomposition of labyrinth and Centaur in their materiality help human beings think about questions of navigation, discovery, the relation between human and animal, and the nature of belief. Fundamentally, as Calasso has said it is about metamorphoses — 'If the power of metamorphosis was to be maintained, there was no alternative but to invent objects and generate monsters'.[27] These objects and monsters are imaginative phenomena but they couldn't be more specific

---

24 Robert Ackerman, *The Myth and Ritual School: J. G. Frazer and the Cambridge Ritualists* (New York: Routledge, 2002) and Walter Burkert, *Structure and History in Greek Mythology and Ritual* (Berkeley: University of California Press, 1979).

25 Edward Said, 'On Repetition', in *The World, the Text, and the Critic* (London: Vintage, 1991), 111–25; Jeffrey Mehlman, *Revolution and Repetition: Marx/Hugo/Balzac* (Berkeley: University of California Press, 1977); Joseph Hillis Miller, *Fiction and Repetition: Seven English Novels* (Oxford: Basil Blackwell, 1982).

26 Cathy Gere, *Knossos and the Prophets of Modernism* (Chicago: Chicago University Press, 2009) and George Thomson, *Aeschylus and Athens: A Study in the Social Origins of Drama* (London: Lawrence and Wishart, 1973).

27 Calasso, *Marriage*, 12.

and material in their manifestation as physical structures and entities. They exist but they represent relations and forces that did not, or do not anymore, exist. They are Never Never lands, but ones that we live within all of the time, almost as if we were the ones held captive in Fairyland.

chapter two

Looking for centaurs

> ...the animal is not the ancestral past, the stone guest, the mute enigma, but the future of man: it is a place, and a threshold, from which man can only be stimulated in view of a more complex and open elaboration of his humanitas
> —Roberto Esposito[1]

The human, as a concept of being human, emerged in Ionia. Human practice and reflections similar to those taking place in Ionia emerged elsewhere. But the human was a fragile and fluid entity and there were different levels and classifications of humanness. Some humans were combined with gods, some were classified as subhuman slaves, some were simply not citizens of a specific *city-state*, still others were cast out into the marginal territories between states. Their bodies became marginal. Other bodies were cast by sculptors or witches into stone and sustained their material existence in marble. Others became objects in other ways. As Page duBois has said of the classical body—'This understanding of human being is somehow imperceptibly inscribed into enduring ways of thinking—about politics, about others, about our own bodies, about

---

1   Roberto Esposito, 'Politics and Human Nature', trans. Lorenzo Chiesa, *Angelaki: Journal of the theoretical humanities* 16, no. 3 (2011): 77–84, 84.

material existence'.² The female Bacchae, the Maenads, confused the boundaries of gods and humans, madness and order, as they performed the rites of Dionysus. Other humans shaded into combination and assemblage with other creatures. Some became half animal in spirit and body, hybrids who fought with and loved humans and animals. Others wanted to dissolve themselves into the being they loved. The human body and its human nature was inherently one of instability.³

Roberto Calasso, in his imaginative reworking of classical mythology, has argued that the proliferation of beings is designed to construct an audience for the activities of the gods. The development of species is the beginning at the first attempts at the *social*, the collectivity. For Calasso,

> In the solitude of the primordial world, the affairs of the gods took place on an empty stage, with no watching eyes to mirror them. There was a rustling, but no clamor of voices. Then, from a certain point on (but at what point? And why?), the backdrop began to flicker, the air was invaded by a golden sprinkling of new beings, the shrill, high-pitched cry of scores of raised voices. Dactyls, Curetes, Corybants, Telchines, Silens, Cabiri, Satyrs, Maenads, Bacchants, Lenaeans, Thyiads, Bassarides, Mimallones, Naiads, Nymphs, Titires: who were all these beings? To evoke one of their names is to evoke them all. They are the helpers, ministers, guardians, nurses, tutors, and spectators of the gods. The

---

2   Page duBois, *Slaves and Other Objects* (Chicago: University of Chicago Press, 2003), 6.
3   Charles Freeman, *The Greek Achievement: The Foundation of the Western World* (Harmondsworth: Allen Lane, 1999), 261.

metamorphic vortex is placated; once surrounded by this noisy and devoted crowd, the gods agree to settle down into their familiar forms. Sometimes that crowd will appear as a pack of murderers, sometimes as an assembly of craftsmen, sometimes as a dance troupe, sometimes as a herd of beasts. That worshipping crowd was the first community, the first group, the first entity in which one name was used for everybody. We don't even know whether they are gods, *daímones*, or human beings. But what is it that unites them, what makes them a single group, even when different and distant from one another? They are the initiated, the ones who have seen.[4]

Judith Barringer has argued that materiality and visuality was central to Greek classical civilisation.[5] The manifestation of the hybrid being of the Centaur, perhaps as a cultural import from the near east,[6] was an explicit visualisation of a crisis in the nature of the human being. What Barringer calls the 'ubiquitous Centauromachy' is a display of multiple meanings and collisions.[7] The most famous Centauromachy visualisations are the Parthenon and the temple of Zeus at Olympia but there are others, largely depicting the war between the Centaurs and their human enemies the Lapiths. The Centauromachy is situated mythologically in the rioting Centaur tribes of Thessaly. The Centaurs are depicted as accurately as the human beings

---

4 Roberto Calasso, *The Marriage of Cadmus and Harmony*, trans. Tim Parks (New York: Alfred A. Knopf, 1993), 302.
5 Judith M. Barringer, *The Art and Archaeology of Ancient Greece* (Cambridge: Cambridge University Press, 2014), 5.
6 Barringer, *Art and Archaeology*, 91.
7 Judith M. Barringer, *Art, Myth and Ritual in Classical Greece* (Cambridge: Cambridge University Press, 2008), 2.

in the relief sculptures. The '*half-human/half-equine*'[8] are represented architecturally in the Parthenon and at Olympia, but Barringer argues for a complex and nuanced understanding of their function — 'What is striking is the malleability of these myths and their meanings, especially the Centauromachy, and their depictions in a great variety of places and contexts'.[9] The very fluidity of the myth replicates the fluidity of the human/equine bodies that are its source. The fact that the Centauromachy becomes one of the central defining features of Olympia and the Parthenon, far beyond its localised and provincial (even barbaric) Thessalian origin, denotes its significance for the classical world and the buildings they made. The archaic origins of the Centaur motifs were undefined, but the motifs were sustained all the way through into late antiquity and the medieval world. Their replication across generations may have been the consequence of seeing other Centaur motifs, in the flesh as it were (in stone in reality), but more likely they were the productions of a specific sense of textuality — people either read about them in a text, or heard about them through oral transmission. The surprising element here is their very specificity and detail. The ornamental and complex elaborations of the hybrid being were profoundly detailed as if they were taken from a real being.

The Lapiths and the Centaurs went to war not because they were strangers to one another but because of their affinities and relatedness. The Centauromachy displays a wedding that they were invited to together until the rioting on the part of the Centaurs began. The Lapiths themselves were certainly a recognised Achaean people for Homer having sent forty manned

---

8 Barringer, *Art, Myth and Ritual*, 23.
9 Barringer, *Art, Myth and Ritual*, 203.

ships to the siege of Troy. The remarkable necropolis of Hellenistic Sidon, now in the Istanbul Archaeology Museum, displays the submission of Lapith to the warring Centaurs, their kindred species.

Klaus Junker has noted that any understanding of classical myth has to engage with the fragmentary nature of images and texts and their relation in a 'discourse of images'.[10] Junker argues for a deeper understanding of the pictorial representations of the Chiron and Achilles myth and the Centauromachy. With recent understandings of photography we have come to think of a visual form as a 'reproduced' image of a specific reality or moment.[11] The image of the Centaur is specific but not a concrete manifestation or direct representation of a real object, unless that real object was the prior sculptural or textual rendition of the entity. Both Junker and Barringer note that originally the Centaurs might have been mistaken versions of a 'remembered reality' of Persians on horseback with the Lapiths representing the Ionians.[12] But the Centauromachy says more about the Ionians than Persians. For Junker,

> To see mythological images as instruments for reflection, literally 'mirroring', is by contrast to understand them as stimuli for one's own intellectual processes and not as confirmation of already existing attitudes. To stay with the example just used: do not the wild centaurs, it has

---

10 Klaus Junker, *Interpreting the Images of Greek Myths: An Introduction*, trans. Annemarie Künzl-Snodgrass and Anthony Snodgrass (Cambridge: Cambridge University Press, 2012), xi–xii. See also Anthony Snodgrass, *Homer and the Artists: Text and Picture in Early Greek Art* (New York: Cambridge University Press, 1998).

11 Junker, *Interpreting the Images*, 40.

12 Junker, *Interpreting the Images*, 188–89.

been asked, in the final analysis represent the impulsive and uncontrollable element that is also part of human nature? The portrayal of the Centauromachy cannot then be reduced to the simple equation, 'We against you' or 'The standard and good against the non-standard and bad.' Rather, it appears as an allegory of characteristics that all form part of the viewers themselves and present them with a mirror — a mirror, admittedly, that does not reflect the surface of things, but makes visible the deeper levels.[13]

The mirror of the Centauromachy, then, reflects not the concrete, specific reality of an origin but mirrors ourselves indirectly. But this is a mirror of what Steiner has called our 'inward lives', reflecting not the actuality and empirical surface of our bodies but the contested, hybrid elements struggling to submerge others or desire others within our psyche. *Hybris*, the improper transgression of boundaries, is the theme of the Centauromachy — an ideological device to delineate the borders of the human and the animal and associate the rioting Centaurs with disorder and lawlessness.[14] Understanding the borderlands of chaos has come to be part not of aesthetic sculptural renditions that somehow materialise the workings of the inner world and the deepest stratified level, but of converse and explication through the analysis of 'psyche'. As if we can find rioting Centaurs there.

But this is if we consider the Centauromachy as a metaphor carrying over meaning about us. But what if the fragmentary remnants of the Centaur are metonymic — with the fragments

---

13 Junker, *Interpreting*, 189.
14 Junker, *Interpreting*, 190.

representing their own beings rather than the turmoil of our inwardness? How far could we track those fragments and signs strewn across Olympia in order to understand Centaurs? Are there ways of methodologically measuring and describing Centaurs as if they were real beasts? They are indeed half-human so at least half of our methods might be appropriate.

Carlo Ginzburg has argued for a historical practice that can reconstruct beings through the tiniest fragments they have left behind — earlobes, fingernails, shapes of fingers and toes.[15] The reconstruction is like the semiotic operations of hunters. As Ginzburg notes,

> Man has been a hunter for thousands of years. In the course of countless chases he learned to reconstruct the shapes and movements of his invisible prey from tracks on the ground, broken branches, excrement, tufts of hair, entangled feathers, stagnating odors. He learned to sniff out, record, interpret, and classify such infinitesimal traces as trails of spittle. He learned how to execute complex mental operations with lightning speed, in the depth of a forest or in a prairie with its hidden dangers.[16]

We know that the fragments of Centaurs are a constantly recurring feature of cultural history — so how can we track and hunt them across history? There are no fossil records of Centaurs, no archaeological stratification that reveals their 'once-existent' status. Two visual pieces by Bill Willers, emeritus professor of biology at University of Wisconsin-Oshkosh, display this status

---

15 Carlo Ginzburg, *Myths, Emblems, Clues*, trans. John and Anne C. Tedeschi (London: Hutchinson Radius, 1990), 96–97.
16 Ginzburg, *Myths, Emblems, Clues,* 102.

of non-existence. Both the 'Centaur of Tymfi' and the 'Excavation at Volos' are faked archaeological specimens—hybrid bone-structures of horse and human being which display the liminal, transitional moment between species. Beauvais Lyons even notes that an exhibition guide told stories that the Volos Centaur was captured by a group of 'Centaur hunting' students in the 1920s.[17] It is the biological specificity and materiality of these structures that point to the fact that these classical repetitions are profoundly detailed and are presented as if they are 'real' beings. But it might be the case that we can understand the specificity of the Centaur as if it were metaphorically rather than literally an archaeological specimen. In that case we would have to consider the human mind and cultures as akin to strata in which we can excavate forms and beings.

In the same manner Erich Kissing's Centaur cycle of paintings (1993–2014) have the same hyper-real aspect—detailed, realistic depictions of the Centaur and groups of Centaurs embedded in contexts of conversation or play. They are quite the opposite of an opaque, aesthetic expressionism. These are literally humans and horses combined into something new. Classical depictions of the Centaur revel in this detail. The visualisation of the non-existent is so specific precisely because it is possible to draw a being from nature because of its status as an assembled or composite entity. We could begin to call these reproductions corporealism—the resurrection and detailed reconstruction of precise corporeal entities (albeit ones which never existed in actuality). The detail and precision of corporealist phantasms is often because we understand their being by filling it out with the detail of us but also because they are

---

17 Beauvais Lyons, 'Subversive Public Art: The Centaur Excavations at Volos', *Number* 64 (2009): 8–9, 8.

conjured up as if they were real to us time and time again. They look like real but impossible bodies.

The Old Centaur and the Young Centaur collectively known as the marble Furietti were found at the villa of Hadrian at Tivoli in the eighteenth century. They are copies of earlier Greek bronze statues from the second century BC and reside in the Capitoline museum with copies in other museums throughout Europe. The copy of the Old Centaur in the Louvre still has a teasing Cupid upon its back. The centaurs have constantly delighted and bemused scholars specifically around the emotions indicated by the Centaurs themselves.[18]

The other great statue in the Capitoline is the equestrian statue of Marcus Aurelius which once stood in the Piazza del Campidoglio. It shows the emperor astride his horse bestowing peace upon his people and displays a relationship between man and horse in combination, affinity and mutuality. Why is one a visual production of an existent, the other of a non-existent? Both Aurelius and Centaur have a material specificity, both are replicated from earlier versions, both are enshrined in textual as much as sculptural production. There are testaments to the existence of the Centaur just as there are to Marcus Aurelius but one exists only in imagination, the other in 'actual history'. Further, what kinds of texts and images furnished the workplaces of those sculptors if the sculpture was not taken from life? The dead and the monstrous and the machine can be thought of as appendices to those things that 'live'. They are a counter-archive of our history of real beings, displaying and distorting our needs, our existential horror about who we are,

---

18 Jon Van de Grift, 'Tears and Revel: The Allegory of the Berthouville Centaur Scyphi', *American Journal of Archaeology* 88 (1984): 377–88.

our compulsions to desire monstrous things.[19] But who are the Centaur remnants archiving against and why do they emerge time and time again? Does the danger of mixed and hybrid beings in the border countries of chaos threaten the very stability of civilisations and states and peoples? Is Faerie and the Never land the recourse of rebels against civilisation and for chaos?

At one and the same time the mixed being is about suppression and production. Its remnants have been scattered in thought and texts across the multiple strata of human culture. But they emerge from the wreckage all of the time. This imaginary as a social-historical production has produced material entities which themselves refer to a non-existent ontology of mixed beings. Cornelius Castoriadis locates the Centaur in thought and in the essentially productive rather than destructive capacity of the human imaginary:

> 'Centaur' is a word that refers to an imaginary being distinct from this word, a being that can be 'defined' by words (by this trait it resembles a pseudo-concept) or represented by images (by this trait it resembles a pseudo-object of perception). But even this easy and superficial example (the imaginary Centaur is only a recombination of pieces taken from real beings) is not exhausted by these considerations, because, for the culture that experienced the mythological reality of the Centaurs, their being was something other than the verbal description or the sculpted representation that could

---

19 See Jeffrey Jerome Cohen, *Of Giants: Sex, Monsters, and the Middle Ages* (Minneapolis: University of Minnesota Press, 1999) and *Medieval Identity Machines* (Minneapolis: University of Minnesota Press, 2003).

be given of them. But how are we to get a hold of this final a-reality? In a certain sense, like the 'thing-in-itself', it offers itself only on the basis of its consequences, its results, its derivatives. How can we grasp God, as an imaginary signification, except on the basis of the shadows (*Abschattungen*) projected onto the effective social action of a people — but, at the same time, how could we overlook that, just like the thing perceived, he is the condition for the possibility of an inexhaustible series of such shadows, but, unlike the thing perceived, he is never given 'in person'?[20]

The '*Abschattungen*' of social action describe the profound processes by which the derivative and the repetition are inscribed in the social practice of the human world, a 'life-world' which imagines entities that have and had no life at all except in the hybrid, composite imagination of those humans looking for some thing at the heart of the labyrinth, itself the imaginary derivative of other multiple mazes.[21] The semantic human/animal frames of the Centaur change, they are unstable and mean different things in differing histories and locations.

The history of the visual form of the Centaur has then to understand the production of visual hybridity and its relation to the human, its visual precision and specificity, and its mode of repeated generation and function. A related question lies

---

20 Cornelius Castoriadis, *The Imaginary Institution of Society*, trans. Kathleen Blamey (Cambridge: Polity, 1987), 141–42.
21 For Castoriadis on the classical world, see Nana Biluš Abaffy, 'The Radical Tragic Imaginary: Castoriadis on Aeschylus and Sophocles', *Cosmos and History: The Journal of Natural and Social Philosophy* 8, no. 2 (2012): 34–59, and Suzi Adams, *Castoriadis's Ontology: Being and Creation* (New York: Fordham University Press, 2011).

in the status of the Centaur as a humanly produced *Daedalian* artefact — those things made not by gods but by human beings themselves. In this sense Daedalus is the maker and creator of Labyrinths and automata. He does not himself produce the Daedalic sculptures of subsequent generations but he does, in mythology, produce his own structures, objects, and beings. Often this is hybrid, like the machinery he constructs for himself and Icarus, based on the observation of the flight of birds or the automata — constructions of both flesh and machine with which he populated his workshops.

The human social-historical production of the hybrid being is itself echoed by the constant attempt on behalf of humans to construct themselves repeatedly as hybrids — beginning with Daedalus and Icarus and their humanly engineered wings — and continued in the search for machine extensions and prosthetics which would exponentially develop their capacity for power and combination in new assemblages. For Tim Ingold, beings (as in existents) and the 'organism' (animal or human) should be understood not as a bounded entity surrounded by an environment but as an unbounded entanglement. For Ingold, the production of the imaginary entity is exactly that which is produced by lines where each being 'is' its story:

> Often the name of the creature is itself a condensed story, so that in its very utterance, the story is carried on. But it is carried on, too, in the calls or vocalizations of the creatures themselves — if they have a voice — as well as in their manifest, visible presence and activity. As a node or knot in a skein of depictions, stories, calls, sightings, and observations, none more 'real' than any other, every creature is not so much a living thing as

the instantiation of a certain way of being alive, each of which, to the medieval mind, would open up a pathway to the experience of God.²²

Imaginary beings, for Ingold, 'are sequestered in a zone of apparitions and illusions that is rigorously partitioned from the domain of real life'.²³ This was a zone prior to the visual taxonomies and classifications of the Enlightenment and one produced by the very concept of the story — 'To track an animal in the book of nature was like following a line of text. But just as the introduction of word-spacing broke the line into segments, so also — in the book of nature — creatures began to appear as discrete, bounded entities rather than as ever-extending lines of becoming'.²⁴ The replacement of the 'becoming of lines' by the fixed, bounded entity finally banishes the fictive beings from our world, as the 'lived reality' of them disappears. It also further creates a sense of the human as an entity whose self-compositions and self-composites become lived in engineering and not just imagination — the dreams of actual hybrid, composite structures move on from 'a-reality' and mythology.

Further, this very displacement of the lived mythological reality of the fictive being does not mean its diminishment. Its multiple productions continue — within the human being itself. As Marx has noted, the fictions, phantasms, and ghosts of the dead 'seize the living' — a process of 'world-historical necromancy' in which old, fictive forms inhabit human beings.²⁵ The

---

22 Tim Ingold, 'Dreaming of Dragons: On the Imagination of Real Life', *Journal of the Royal Anthropological Institute* 19 (2013): 734–52, 741.
23 Ingold, 'Dreaming', 736.
24 Ingold, 'Dreaming', 743.
25 Karl Marx and Friedrich Engels, *Collected Works, Volume 11: 1851–1853* (London: Lawrence and Wishart, 1979), 104.

semantic productions of these beings in different circumstances of course make questionable the sense of origin and what these motifs did 'actually' mean. This is not our question, but it is still one which exercises detectives and scholars who try and excavate, both culturally and physically (as in Schliemann's Troy), the Never lands of the classical past.

Recently, Carlo Ginzburg has looked for a rational cause for the multiple cultural production of the Centaur. Noting that the motif may be of Scythian origin denoting humans on horseback, it also refers to equine and wolf-like hybrids as part of a system of periodic animal/human metamorphosis.[26] Robert Graves has argued for an origin of the Centaur in a sacred form of the hobby-horse dance — the earliest Greek representation found on a Mycenaean gem from the Heraeum at Argos depicting two men joined at the waist to horse's bodies and dancing. At the same time he also notes the vestiges of the Centaur as representative of a real or mythological people such as the Scythians or the pre-Hellenic Albanian population, as well as Persians in other accounts.[27]

Cultural theorists such as René Girard have tried to understand the specificity of the horse and the man which has been entwined together in the 'monstrous metamorphosis' of the Centaur. This is important for understanding the historical presence and absence of the Centaur. Since it is an 'imaginary' beast in the sense that it is imagined and conjured up (from the remnants of a real being) rather than merely fictional (having never existed), there is no limit to its metamorphosis or its

---

26 Carlo Ginzburg, *Ecstasies: Deciphering the Witches Sabbath* (Harmondsworth: Penguin, 1991).
27 Robert Graves, *The Greek Myths, Volume Two* (London: Pelican, 1960), 209–10.

resurrection. Within the 'monstrous whole' of the Centaur as a category, there is an infinity of individual monsters without stability as shapes. The icon's very dissolution and dispersal are the premise upon which the infinitude of the icon across time and space is founded. The birth of monsters is made possible by its dissolving, hybrid status. Phenomenologically, it has neither existence as an entity already pre-existing in the soul, nor is it a reflection in the mind of a reality external to the mind.[28] It is this ambivalent status of an existing, non-existing phenomena that George Steiner writes of when he notes that 'A Centaur is a hyphen between manifest realities'.[29] The manifest realities of human and horse become questioned in their combination and in the dissolution of the borders between them.

As Castoriadis notes on the precision of the visual representation — 'There is an "essence" of the Centaur: two definite sets of possibilities and of impossibilities. This "essence" is "representable": there is nothing imprecise about the "generic" physical appearance of the Centaur.'[30] Even in its moment of instability and dissolution the template of the Centaur still has some fixity — there is a limit to the manipulation of its component parts. The artefact of the Centaur is a sensual object that we come upon and recompose sensually, but can that observation delineate the 'essence' of the Centaur or just its necessary and defining qualities and properties that have to be present for it to be depicted?

---

28 René Girard, 'Myth and Ritual in Shakespeare: A Midsummer Night's Dream', in *Textual Strategies: Perspectives in Post-Structuralist Criticism*, ed. J.V. Harari (London: Methuen, 1980), 207.
29 George Steiner, *Real Presences* (London: Faber, 1989), 202.
30 Cornelius Castoriadis, *The Imaginary Institution of Society*, trans. Kathleen Blamey (Cambridge: Polity, 1987), 391n51.

The very materiality of the Centaur hints at those sculptural artefacts signifying a set of invisible properties for the cultures who live them, and in describing these properties we might be able to describe why these recursive moments are so compelling for human beings. For Castoriadis 'A visible object may possess invisible properties; a stone or an animal may be a god; a child may be the reincarnation of an ancestor or this very ancestor in person. It may be that these attributes, properties, relations, forms of being are lived, spoken, thought and enacted in sincerity, duplicity or (in our eyes) utter confusion'.[31] The search for the social relations invested in aesthetic form is always problematic. But the production and re-production of these visual formations and objects as part of the creation of the social-historical mean that they are profoundly social objects, and ones which problematize the very notion of a human science as the production of human beings. The idea that an object has within its entity invisible properties has two implications — whether those properties emerge from the observed being of an object (and whether this is possible) or whether those properties are imposed upon or associated with the object from without. If the stone has the invisible property of divinity — is this enshrined in the very being of the object or imposed from without? Or the child as carrier of another soul? The transmigratory and unstable character of souls in the classical world, invested in stone and wood and in other beings, might seem archaic but those very processes of investment and association still continue in our cultures and our imaginaries.

One of the ways of understanding the human entity is to think about its invisible properties and the kinds of mirrors

---

31 Castoriadis, *Imaginary Institution*, 227.

that might reflect and refract the 'inwardness' of that being. The geological analogy of human beings with strata illustrates that sense of the invisible properties of the human in the same way as mechanistic modes of thinking associated living beings and brains with machines in the classical world, or humans as the products of elements, weather, vapours, and so on.

Suzi Adams argues that when Castoriadis sees the human being he sees it as a stratified entity — 'one that creates itself in irregular, heterogenous strata'. In this vein, the lines of continuity and discontinuity between anthropic and natural regions of being were redrawn, and, as part of that, a phenomenology of life emerges via his reactivation of ancient Greek images of the world, and his reconsideration of time and creation as they pertained to the living being and the physical world'.[32] Humans, like nature, are self-altered forms and strata.[33] As forms of strata, Adams argues that Castoriadis elaborates upon 'the lines of continuity between human and non-human Worlds'.[34] We see the lines of continuity between the human and the non-human, at the same time as we see the breaks between them. Who could separate the equine and the human in the being of the Centaur — where is the seam between them? How do we separate the human as a product and self-product of nature and her social being?[35] Certainly in the account of the Lapith war in Ovid's *Metamorphoses* the Centaur is noted as protecting both his human- and his horse-being in the fight. But the

---

32 Suzi Adams, 'Towards a *Post*-Phenomenology of Life: Castoriadis' Critical Naturphilosophie', *Cosmos and History: The Journal of Natural and Social Philosophy* 4 (2008): 1–2, 387–400, 389.
33 Adams, '*Post*-Phenomenology', 393.
34 Adams, '*Post*-Phenomenology', 399.
35 See Sébastien Douchet, 'La Peau du centaure à la frontière de l'humanité et de l'animalité', *Micrologus* 13 (2005): 285–312.

exact seams or differences between the human and equine elements were a source of some commentary in the medieval proliferation of Centaur accounts and visualisations, specifically around the incompatibility of its variant units. The meeting points of species undermine the idea of human difference, but also display the lines of contestation between human and non-human.[36]

To continue the analogy of the strata; if we see the human as stratified where do we locate the Centaur within those strata? Further, to use an archaeological analogy as we talk about sedimentation and burial — how can we archaeologically excavate the Centaur out of those strata knowing that we will find only invented, fabricated, fictional phenomena? Mike Pearson and Michael Shanks have examined the idea of unearthing the strata in their work on theatre, the classical, and archaeology:

> An artefact, as is accepted, is a multitude of data points, an infinity of possible attributes and measurements. Which ones are made and held to constitute its identity depends conventionally upon method and the questions being asked by the archaeologist. But we also hold that the artefact is itself a multiplicity. Its identity is multiple. It is not just one thing. The artefact does not only possess a multitude of data attributes, but is also itself multiplicity. We come to an object in relationships with

---

36 See Giorgio Agamben, *The Open: Man and Animal*, trans. Kevin Attell (Stanford: Stanford University Press, 2004), Donna Haraway, *When Species Meet* (Minneapolis: University of Minnesota Press, 2008), and John Hartigan, *Aesop's Anthropology: A Multispecies Approach* (Minneapolis: University of Minnesota Press, 2015).

it, through using, perceiving it, referring to it, talking of it, feeling it as something.[37]

The material artefact of the archaeological excavation is a multiplicity of data points. It is sensual even when the questions we ask of it do not mark the being of the object in itself or even elaborate what it is. It is like the questions asked by others of Odysseus — whatever they ask, we do not understand Odysseus as a multiplicity. Neither do we exhaust the possibility of the excavated object. The Centaur, locked in the mental strata (and their aesthetic productions) of the human being is itself a multiplicity of invisible and visible properties — neither dependent on what we ask of it nor independent of human creation.

But what do humans as strata mean for self-creation of human beings themselves? On the one hand we have the stratified human consciousness of individual human beings, on the other the stratified consciousness of peoples and civilisations, even of the whole of humanity. Each stratum laid upon the one below, the archaic vestiges of earlier versions of humanity perhaps accessible through excavation, method, surveying, and the questions we ask of it. But human beings are themselves strewn across stratified systems of geological time, immersed in rock and soil. They are also strewn across the strata of our imaginary histories and elaborations, each stratum providing the matrices, resources, and templates for further elaborations and repetitions of what has gone before. No wonder that as people excavated their history and who they were (and wanted to be), they found the collision and combination in the strata

---

[37] Mike Pearson and Michael Shanks, *Theatre/Archaeology* (London: Routledge, 2001), 99.

of different human types. Perhaps human beings melded with stone or animals, the seams between them unapparent or undetectable. Perhaps they were even born of stone or dust as in the creation myths of some peoples or like the folklore of swallows, locked in rock, and only emerging in spring. But there are also the places where human beings walked, the places they built.

The question of the animal as the future of the human, which Esposito notes, opens up a more generous and expansive concept of the human. This might be about the dissolution of boundaries or the displacement or de-centring of the human. But it might also be about extending human possibilities in a more radicalised humanism which combines, contests, conglomerates rather than dissolves the human, like a metamorphosis that submerges the human being into another entity or topples it from the lofty height of the classification of nature and its strata.

chapter three

Surveying the labyrinth

> We cannot do without reason — even though we know its insufficiency, its limitations. And, exploring these, we are again within reason — while of reason itself we can give neither account nor reasons. We are not, for that, blind or lost. We are able to elucidate what we think, what we are. Having created our Labyrinth, we survey it, bit by bit.
> —Cornelius Castoriadis[1]

Klaus Junker, in his study of mythological discourse, has argued that when we see Ariadne, we build the absent world around her — 'Theseus as recipient of the thread, the walls of the labyrinth'.[2] There are walls and corridors around our Centaurs, Minotaurs and Ariadnes. These are lost walls, imagined Never Never land walls — sometimes the *half-remembered* reality of a place long gone, sometimes an utter fabrication. Again: *This* is where the Achaean camp was, *this* is where Agamemnon slept. No design, plan, or building has been dispersed more than the labyrinth enclosing Ariadne, designed and built by the hands

---

1 Cornelius Castoriadis, *Crossroads in the Labyrinth* (Brighton: Harvester Press, 1984), xxviii.
2 Klaus Junker, *Interpreting the Images of Greek Myths: An Introduction*, trans. Annemarie Künzl-Snodgrass and Anthony Snodgrass (Cambridge: Cambridge University Press, 2012), 46.

of a human. It has proliferated as a metaphor for the human condition, another mirror of our inward lives, as if below our surface we have the *meander*, the circuitous pathways in which we are lost. But the labyrinth, perhaps as an echo of the labyrinthine and circuitous lanes of Troy, is materially *re-invested* and recomposed throughout subsequent history. It is rebuilt time and time again.[3]

The classical visual motif of the labyrinth recurs across many cultures and materially emerges in a number of ways; medieval and post-medieval landscape designs, in cathedrals and churches as a decorative ritual device, in contemporary art and design, in manuscripts.[4] The social-historical production of the labyrinth motif has its ultimate origins in a series of classical tales including Theseus, Ariadne, and the Labyrinth of Minos, and in the Achaean assault upon Troy, where the walls of Troy and their navigation leads to the centre of the city and the ensuing victory against the Trojans — Helen as a ghost at the heart of it. Robert Graves elucidates the Ariadne myth:

> Now, before Daedalus left Crete, he had given Ariadne a magic ball of thread, and instructed her how to enter and leave the Labyrinth. She must open the entrance door and tie the loose end of the thread to the lintel; the ball would then roll along, diminishing as it went and making, with devious turns and twists, for the innermost recess where the Minotaur was lodged. This ball

---

[3] See W.H. Matthews, *Mazes and Labyrinths: A General Account of their History and Developments* (London: Longmans, Green, 1922) and *Mazes and Labyrinths: Their History and Development* (New York: Dover, 1970).

[4] Jeff Saward, *Magical Paths: Labyrinths and Mazes in the 21st Century* (London: Mitchell Beazley, 2002) and Jeff Saward, *Labyrinths and Mazes: The Definitive Guide to Ancient and Modern Traditions* (London: Gaia Books, 2003).

Ariadne gave to Theseus, and instructed him to follow it until he reached the sleeping monster, whom he must seize by the hair and sacrifice to Poseidon. He could then find his way back by rolling up the thread into a ball again.[5]

The Minotaur was Ariadne's half-brother. In return for rescuing Theseus he took her away but then abandoned her (to her many incarnations and many deaths). Graves in his notes refers to the discovery of 'Cretan' mazes in Cornwall scratched upon walls and links the maze structure to Celtic ritual myth as well as the dissemination of the trope in the flight from Troy.

Some historical Scandinavian and British labyrinths are explicitly called 'Troytown', 'Walls of Troy', or 'Trojeberg'.[6] Although many of these 'Troytowns' still exist, some have disappeared. They may once have been a ubiquitous feature of the landscape. 'The Walls of Troy' labyrinth near Dalby in North Yorkshire is a classic version of the seven-circuit classical labyrinth cut into turf and recut due to road damage around 1900. It is still used by children to navigate their way into the centre of the structure. The idea of the 'Troytown' is also central to Cornish labyrinth structures[7] where, as Nigel Pennick notes, the turf or stone maze of the 'Troys' mean a 'house in disorder' in Cornish dialect.[8] It is also perceived by its users as a game of

---

5   Robert Graves, *The Greek Myths (Combined Edition)* (Harmondsworth: Penguin, 1992), 339.
6   Penelope Reed Doob, *The Idea of the Labyrinth: From Classical Antiquity through the Middle Ages* (Ithaca: Cornell University Press, 1990), 232.
7   Morton R. Nance, 'Troy Town', *Journal of the Royal Institute of Cornwall* 71 (1924): 262–79.
8   Nigel Pennick, *Mazes and Labyrinths* (London: Robert Hale, 1990), 191.

'Troy',[9] where social practices and operations are performed around the navigation of the structure reminiscent of its mythical ritual status. In fact, the idea of the visual Troy motif as a method of serendipitous navigation can be seen in the Welsh 'Caerdroia' and 'Caer y troiau' literally meaning the 'city of turns' or the 'city of turnings'.[10] Itself a potential memory remnant of the Arthurian motif of the automata of the 'turning castle'.

The idea of a house in disorder, reminiscent of the multiple sedimentations and stratifications of Schliemann's Troy, is noted by Doob in her cultural history of what she calls the 'Daedalian domus' or house of Daedalus, the builder of the Cretan labyrinth.[11] The extension of the idea of the dwelling into a building structure was itself put forward by Borges in the idea of the library of Babel as labyrinth,[12] where the tower of Babel itself as a visualised manifestation of the will to human knowledge and understanding is itself condemned to a labyrinth of multiple languages. For Bloch in his speculative mathematics of the labyrinth of Borges there might even be a 'grammar of an ideal logic capable of straightening out the labyrinth in which we found ourselves'.[13]

Janet Bord has also documented the mythological status of the visualised labyrinth as one of ghosts — specifically

---

9   Pennick, *Mazes and Labyrinths*, 23.
10 Pennick, *Mazes and Labyrinths*, 36, 59.
11 Doob, *The Idea of the Labyrinth*, xii, 97.
12 Jorge Luis Borges, *Labyrinths: Selected Stories and Other Writings* (Harmondsworth: Penguin, 1970), 78, and George Steiner, *After Babel: Aspects of Language and Translation* (Oxford: Oxford University Press, 1975), 71–73.
13 William Goldbloom Bloch, *The Unimaginable Mathematics of Borges' Library of Babel* (Oxford: Oxford University Press, 2008), 106.

providing maps to the underworld and the pathways of the dead.[14] Nigel Pennick has also found a correlation between the siting of labyrinths near gallows hills[15] which may be due to the liminal locations on the borders between the living and the dead where the visuality of the labyrinth acts as a porous, permeable, and transitional geography. As Pennick notes — 'The tangled threads formed a protective border which was believed to bridge the material and the non-material worlds, creating an entanglement that evil spirits could not penetrate'.[16] This is something that Ingold points to in his discussion of the 'apotropaic' patterns of mazes suggested by the work of Alfred Gell. These patterns are structured in order to confuse demons and protect sheltering beings from evil spirits. Ingold argues that in apotropaic patterning systems demons become fascinated with the unravelling of and solutions to puzzles but will fail always to solve the problem of the labyrinth — a problem set them by human beings themselves inscribing surfaces.[17] But there is a difference between the human and inhuman observational positions with the demon looking from above at the pattern, as Ingold says,

> Such a perspective, however is not available to the terrestrial traveller who is already embarked upon a journey across the earth's surface — a journey that is tantamount to life itself. The entrance to the maze marks the point not at which he touches down upon the surface,

---

14 Janet Bord, *Mazes and Labyrinths of the World* (London: Latimer New Dimensions, 1976), 10.
15 Pennick, *Mazes and Labyrinths*, 47.
16 Pennick, *Mazes and Labyrinths*, 54.
17 Tim Ingold, *Lines: A Brief History* (London: Routledge, 2007), 53.

but at which he goes underground. Now as an interface of earth and air, the ground is a kind of surface that is visible from above, but not from below. It does not have another side. Thus at the very moment of going underground, of entering the labyrinth, the surface itself disappears from sight. It appears to dissolve. This moment marks the transition from life to death. Thenceforth — and quite unlike Gell's demon which, caught in the contemplation of an apotropaic pattern, is glued to the surface — the ghostly traveller finds himself in a world without any surface at all. Every path is now a thread rather than a trace. And the maze of passages, never visible on its totality, can only be reconstructed by those few — such as the hero Theseus, or the Chukchi shaman who drew the sketch for Bogoras — who have visited the world of the dead and made it back again.[18]

This phenomenology of navigation is in itself made more problematic by a difference in labyrinth structure between those that have multiple routes through (multicursal) and those that have only one (unicursal). The latter as a single navigable route would have no need of Ariadne's thread. The former is more a structure of ritual and pilgrimage. For Nigel Pennick,

> Wherever they have existed, the basic theme of the labyrinths has been that of impenetrability and entrapment. This may be taken literally, in that any person entering the maze is lost. Entering the labyrinth, the individual is 'amazed' by the profusion of pathways, and the faculty of

---

18 Ingold, *Lines*, 56–57.

rational thought is obliterated…Whatever the material of construction may be, there is no generally agreed system of maze and labyrinth classification. However there are certain well-defined categories. Basically, mazes and labyrinths can be divided into two forms, the unicursal, in which there is a single pathway, with no deviations or dead ends, and the multicursal, where there are many paths, which may include dead ends.[19]

Penelope Doob notes that errors and entrapment are at the very centre of the labyrinth experience.[20] 'Labyrinthicity' is not just about visual structures but about concepts and ideas. For Doob the 'Classical labyrinth texts reveal the Labyrinth's duality: embodying both superb design and unfathomable chaos'. Its aesthetic is one of 'equivocal meander', circumlocution, and turning.[21]

F.W. Sieber's sketch of the Gortyna caverns of Crete displays the kinds of complexities and turnings of labyrinthine structures.[22] Gortyna has been perceived as the template of the Minoan labyrinth myth but its natural structures are counterposed to the humanly constructed, designed labyrinths that are created and re-created through human history — and the fact that mythology makes Daedalus, a human, the designer of the maze. This sense of the human is central to understanding the production of the labyrinth by the social-historical but also in understanding it as a profoundly social object. The fact of human design means the capacity to understand the labyrinth

---

19 Pennick, *Mazes and Labyrinths*, 15–16.
20 Doob, *The Idea of the Labyrinth*, xv.
21 Doob, *The Idea of the Labyrinth*, 52–53.
22 Ingold, *Lines*, 54.

as a human and as a socially produced phenomena with all kinds of human and social practices arrayed around it and imposed upon it. Its emergence across multiple spatial and temporal locations means that it 'does something' socially; it has its own logic, rationality, reason.

For Cornelius Castoriadis the labyrinth exemplifies and amplifies something beyond a simple sense of creation; it is the prime analogy of the human and social condition per se and our methodologies for understanding that condition and experience. For Castoriadis, 'We are able to elucidate what we think, what we are. Having created our Labyrinth, we survey it, bit by bit.'[23]

Castoriadis raises three central aspects of 'labyrinthicity'. Firstly, that the labyrinth is the product of human, not divine, beings. As Castoriadis says, 'There can be no doubt that the myth was saying something important when it made the Labyrinth the work of Daedalus, a man.'[24] Secondly, labyrinths and their continual visual production in history point both to repetition and to constant creation, that each may be a version, but those versions are themselves turning and constructing something new both in terms of new circumstances, forces, and relations and for new social practices to be performed upon them. Thirdly, the imaginary within which the idea and practice of the labyrinth takes place is itself a product of thought and to think is to enter the labyrinth; to find ones way, looking for clues, finding the centre, hunting monsters. This is at once a labyrinth of materiality and of thought:

---

23 Castoriadis, *Crossroads*, xxviii.
24 Castoriadis, *Crossroads*, x.

Things are no longer simply juxtaposed: the nearest is the furthest, and the forks on the road, instead of succeeding one another, have become simultaneous, mutually intersecting. The entrance to the Labyrinth is at once one of its centres — or, rather, we no longer know whether there is a centre, what a centre is. Obscure galleries lead away on every side, entangled with others coming from we know not where, going, perhaps, nowhere. We should never have crossed this threshold, we should have stayed outside... The only choice we still keep is to follow this gallery rather than that other into the darkness...[25]

Materiality is inseparable from thought — 'To think is to enter the Labyrinth.'[26] Further there are visual labyrinths that are continually constructed by human beings that are imaginary architectural systems such as mathematics which, although rooted in the logics of nature, create speculative and abstract labyrinths of thought — constructed again by human beings. They are what Castoriadis calls 'Daedalian artefacts'[27] where the whole idea of solving the mystery and getting to the centre becomes part of the vast abstraction of the system. But what does lie at the centre of the unicursal and multicursal labyrinths is the monster to be banished. Certainly in some visualisations on Roman jewels it is the Centaur at the heart of the labyrinth.[28] This gets us to another production of human beings, another Daedalian artefact, and one in which the constant recursiveness

---

25 Castoriadis, *Crossroads*, ix.
26 Castoriadis, *Crossroads*, x.
27 Castoriadis, *Crossroads*, xi.
28 Pennick, *Mazes and Labyrinths*, 40.

of the classical motif and its translation into new forms creates a new way of thinking about the very visual ontology of the human being itself. Why did the myth make the labyrinth the work of a human rather than a god?

The humanly constructed labyrinth is at once a metaphor of the human condition and our knowledge, but also a material mapping of the route to other worlds — specifically the land of the dead. The recursive motif of the labyrinth becomes materialised time and time again in multiple locations as both a ritual and a ludic template for the traverse of human beings. It is built by and for humans themselves. The labyrinth is symbolic but it is also a map of the once existed, never existed. Its routes recall the traverse both to the centre of Troy but also the centre of the palace of Minos. The labyrinth is both a journey of discovery and a prison. These are not just metaphorical journeys but echoes of practices and historical moments. Even when the original labyrinths remain in the netherworld of Never land their constant reproduction and elaboration repeats a gesture or an insight of archaic, classical humanity — that there was a mystery to solve or a place to escape from.

The proliferation of the labyrinth is a consequence of a circular set of copying procedures; that the image becomes circulated and sustained in manuscripts or that people had seen previous versions. This might be serendipitous or it might also point to the migrations of peoples in which the motif was carried. In any case, people in different spatio-temporal locations were trying to solve ludic, existential, and ritual problems through the construction and traverse of labyrinth. Perhaps their building sustained a mystery that could not be transmitted in any other form. But those problems that are aided by the labyrinth may not be the same across all of those times and locations — the labyrinth may just be a serendipitous, if historically sedimented, gift to subsequent generations.

The difference between the unicursal labyrinth and the multicursal hints at the different sets of problems that each might be part of. The unicursal route takes us to the centre as a procession, the multicursal is a much more complex exercise in orientation and navigation; the first perhaps ritual, the second a camp of internment and captivity, loss and despair. There is no need for Ariadne's thread in one version, but we are compelled to its use in the other. The caverns of Gortyna were a complex network of tunnels that led nowhere. They had no centre, or the centre was displaced, or there was no knowing whether one were at the centre or not. Perhaps as we enter the darkness the point is not to find that centre, only to traverse. At the centre of the labyrinth at Chartres there is just nothing there; no monsters, no secrets. Just ourselves having traversed its maze, and perhaps carrying our monsters and secrets there with us.

chapter four

Daedalus and his machines

> The figures of Daedalus, automata, like slaves, existing at the bidding of their master and maker, will always flee if they can.
> —Page duBois[1]

Daedalus is the maker of labyrinths, but he also the maker of sculptures, of automata, of crafts. He makes wings for himself and his son that extend the possibilities of the human and allow escape from the labyrinth. Artefacts and sculptures are named for him.[2] He exemplifies *making*. Daedalus designs, builds, extends, but he also creates imaginary structures that, even though they might be linked to the world of nature, are human constructs and fabrications—like mathematics. Like mathematics, the object he makes is part of a multiply stratified 'ideal' and constructed world that 'encounters' the multiply stratified physical world.[3] The very practice of arithmetic can newly engineer that world of nature, transforming it to make it more suitable human habitations. It can also help to design

---

1 Page duBois, *Slaves and Other Objects* (Chicago: University of Chicago Press, 2003), 248n.
2 For a discussion of Daedalic sculpture, see John Boardman, *Greek Sculpture: The Archaic Period* (London: Thames and Hudson, 1978).
3 Cornelius Castoriadis, *Philosophy, Politics, Autonomy: Essays in Political Philosophy* (Oxford: Oxford University Press, 1991), 27.

the geometric form of the labyrinth to imprison, confuse, mirror ourselves. Arithmetic can also engineer our *post-humanness*, creating new prosthetic human forms and automata. Not only is the labyrinth the work of a man, the work of the same man also enables his and our escape from it. Every produced human artefact is Daedalian, produced and reproduced with its own logics often only tangentially encountering nature.[4] Labyrinths, Centaurs, gods are themselves Daedalian. The Centauromachy is a human construction with its own geometries of explanation and power. Humans make things by replicating nature, animals, other human beings through observation, experimentation, technique.[5]

The imaginary entities of the Centaur and the labyrinth are at once the textual production of story *lines* (appearing as they do in the texts of classical mythology) and as the material production of constantly recurring visual images. In that sense the inhabitation of these texts and images in the imaginary makes possible that constant utilisation of those visual forms in production. They are the matrices of constant human production — the engines and machines which accumulate and produce images and discourses. The textual and visual constitution of those entities are of course not limited to labyrinths or centaurs — those are just exemplars. But each of those exemplars displays something distinctive about a visual architectural form

---

[4] Martyn Hudson and Tim Shaw, 'Dead Logics and Worlds: Sound Art and Sonorous Objects', *Organised Sound* 20, no. 2 (2015): 263–72, and Martyn Hudson, 'Archive, Sound and Landscape in Richard Skelton's *Landings Sequence*', *Landscapes* 16, no. 1 (June 2015): 63–78.

[5] See Bernard Stiegler, *Technics and Time, 1: The Fault of Epimetheus*, trans. Richard Beardsworth and George Collins (Stanford: Stanford University Press, 1998). For Stiegler the *re-visioning* of the Epithemean mythic structures parallels and reworks those of the Promethean.

and a visual biological form, and, in fact, they are forms which are linked by their relation in myth.

Living, designing, and building within that world Daedalus used human engineering in both his labyrinth and to become a hybrid being, a monstrous form that would fly. His knowledge accumulated as part of the life-world makes that design possible — but it is only the 'taking leave' from the world of his son that reaffirms the boundary between human and bird. The hybrid being was destroyed in that process. Hubris may be why the legends of hybridity and building are so compelling — enmeshed as they are in both the potentiality and limitations of human creativity. And not just the creation and recreation of classical motifs or of the world itself but of their own humanity — constantly seeking to design, to transform, to create machines as extensions of the human being.[6] Human beings, like labyrinths and centaurs are collections of lines — for Tim Ingold — 'After all, what is a thing, or indeed a person, if not a tying together of the lines — the paths of growth and movement of all the many constituents gathered there?'[7] Navigating the labyrinths of the human and the world it has constructed of forms, motifs, replications is the task of a history of visual 'existents' and imaginaries.

The idea of Daedalian artefacts as imaginary objects is part of the whole history of the invention of visual forms such as art, architecture, armour, as products of social forces and relations and as structures of signification of the social formation. As Sarah Morris has argued — from the first note of Daedalus in Greek poetry in the *Iliad*, the Daedalus myth is entwined

---

6   Castoriadis, *Philosophy, Politics, Autonomy*, 275.
7   Tim Ingold, *Lines: A Brief History* (London: Routledge, 2007), 5.

with the idea of production.[8] Even if Daedalus himself is a 'literary creation' or a device to be emblematic of drawing, design, building, and production.[9] The importance of the Daedalian artefact as an object rests upon three of its properties; that the artefact is a repetitious assemblage of the social-historical and bears its imprint, and can therefore be described and surveyed; that it is a human rather than a divine or natural production and reproduction; and that the recurrence of the visual Daedalian artefact into multiple spatial, temporal, *epochal* locations bears witness to the primacy of the imaginary in the creation of cultural forms.

The question of the methodological description of the Daedalian artefact is central when there is no such thing as the 'empirical' centaur to be described. The description would have to lie in the analytics of the mode of its multiplicity of production. The status of the artefact as a human production displays its contingency, its situated social meaningfulness (rather than natural or divine meaning), and its utility in divergent epochs. The imaginary use of extra-territorial visual forms is concerned with the endless social use and creation of a limited number of original or Ur-motifs and stories. Describing these properties then has a number of implications for the understanding of visual form.

Firstly, that the description of Daedalian artefacts makes problematic the very issue of realism and the documenting of social existence and phenomena because these are essentially imaginary phenomena even when their products are what we have called corporealist. Examining the composite, recursive

---

8   Sarah P. Morris, *Daidalos and the Origins of Greek Art* (Princeton: Princeton University Press, 1992), 3.
9   Morris, *Daidalos*, xx.

structures of the imaginary means that the description is of derivative, secondary elaborations of an archaic motif going back into antiquity. The 'world-historical necromancy' of archaic forms and entities structures contemporary human relations.

Secondly, the search for a historical 'object' has always been problematic in the classical projects of social science and historical practice. When these forms are aesthetic ones, it makes even more difficult a project of examination and elucidation specifically if one considered the realm of art (the Furietti Centaurs) to be an essentially autonomous, private space in which there is a sense of the privileged visual form, which should not be ransacked for the traces of social relations invested within it. The task of delineating the specifically social features then becomes the project of description — the sense that there is an ontology of objects which make certain types of narrative extraction possible whilst leaving others in the realm of the aesthetic — that art is in a sense untranslatable and that its significations are resistant to social analytics.

Finally, the sense of the object intimates a more general theory of the production of cultural artefacts which delineates the role of labour, production, and creation as being at the heart of the human life-world, at the same time as that human life-world only offers a limited series of cultural forms available for use and recombination. The extra-territoriality of Daedalian artefacts, de-materialised from their spaces and times of origin, intimates that that labour of production is intertwined with the question of the human as a labouring, and specifically storytelling, machine, and that the stories it produces are an attempt to tell the social about its limitations and capacities to produce other types of machines and powers. Unlike this story, that story has no end until the end of the human. And unlike the labyrinth, the human has no one centre, no one mystery to solve — its ghosts speak and recur all of the time.

These three aspects, of the imaginary archaic form and its powers, of the resistance of aesthetic forms to social analytics, and of the nature of the story-telling human, are, however only first steps in thinking about Daedalian artefacts and visual methodologies. We might think that if the labyrinth and the Centaur were built by us, they should not defy or refute our descriptions. In many ways this dissonance between the artefact and the description is still the central problematic in the idea of the historical object. We still want to survey our labyrinths and Centaurs because they were the work of a human being.

The idea of the *work* and *making* of human beings takes us back to what Page duBois has called the 'the fabricated statues of Daedalus, who will run if they can, like slaves who want to be free'.[10] The figures of Daedalus are automata, created and engineered, who are trying to escape their master's will. David Wills has noted what he calls the 'play of artifice' and the artfulness of Daedalian objects in his work on the theories of prosthetics.[11] But these artifices as extensions of the human body (wings), as buildings built from our imagination (labyrinths), and as independent manifestations of our will and craft (automata) also point to something of utter importance for created, hybrid entities — the seams between the natural and the constructed, the birthed and the engineered. The seams between the elements and units which combine to create the assemblages of new structures and beings — beings which mirror both our surfaces and our inwardnesses — are grafts of

---
10 duBois, *Slaves*, 161.
11 David Wills, *Prosthetics* (Stanford: Stanford University Press, 1995), 143.

alien objects. What is the seam that lies between the human and the equine in the Centaur, where is the seam between the human form and the wing attached to Icarus by his father?

Cornelius Castoriadis again can give us some insight into those hybrid, created beings — those Daidala. Human beings are always seamed and grafted — their mode of being is a multiplicity and an ensemble of component parts — our being is a set of strata just like the uncovered city of 'Troy' or of the constituents gathered there.[12] The Daedalian automaton is a speculative being, like the Centaur, its human maker can reproduce one after another. But it is also the self-alteration of the own being of its maker. The maker can preserve its own being in the new form, but also self-reproduce and self-alter. It contains within the principle of both generation and corruption, and can extend this out into other beings and forms.[13] For Castoriadis form can alter itself as form, and the whole idea of closure and ending becomes 'shattered' — 'In other words, man is the only animal capable of breaking the closure in and through which every other living being is'.[14] The self-institution of the human is limited only by her capacity to imagine. The replication of new entities and social forms is itself not simply repetition but constant self-elaboration and self-alteration.

In the *Grundrisse* notebooks of Marx, the machine is subordinate to the capacity for human fabrication — machines are 'the power of knowledge, objectified', organs of human minds

---

12 Cornelius Castoriadis, 'The Logic of Magmas and the Question of Autonomy', in *The Castoriadis Reader*, ed. D.A. Curtis (Oxford: Basil Blackwell, 1997), 290–318, 291.

13 Castoriadis, 'Logic', 309.

14 Castoriadis, 'Logic', 314.

and hands.[15] The self-elaboration and self-alteration of human beings means the production of new automata and new social machines — machines in which the seam between biological organism and engineered automata dissolves.

The question is then not the meaning of the Daedalian artefact but what it means to us. The very shape-shifting of the human form, its indeterminacy and permeability, is also the reason why we create and the grounds for that creation and the genesis of new and repeated elaborations of what it is to be human.

If the human being has its mode of alteration at the heart of its mode of being, then the human is a module of possibilities. It can, as Castoriadis has said, play with its possibilities, extensions, alterations.[16] The classical world is neither petrified nor destroyed, it lives on within our human frames and imaginaries. As George Steiner says — 'New "Antigones" are being imagined, thought, lived now; and will be tomorrow.'[17]

As Page duBois has taught us, the classical world was one of light and darkness. One of its central bequests to us has been slavery and human beings as objects. It was a world of savagery, bestiality, and horror. But it also opened spaces for thought and for art. Its fragmentary literatures, its political ideals live on in our cultures. We see ourselves with Achilles in the Achaean camp, we look for our ancestors in the Antigones of the classical world. The development of the imagined territories of democracy and philosophy are about fabrication — these were

---

15 Karl Marx, *Grundrisse: Foundations of the Critique of Political Economy (Rough Draft)* (Harmondsworth: Penguin, 1973), 706.
16 Castoriadis, *Philosophy, Politics, Autonomy*, 31, 39.
17 George Steiner, *Antigones: The Antigone Myth in Western Literature, Art and Thought* (Oxford: Oxford University Press, 1986), 34.

things made by human beings from the things they found in the world around them. The social relations and political economies of the city-states, their heroic poetry, their mythologies were labyrinths created by the peoples of Ionia to mirror and explore themselves and their world.

The demos and the multitude of the classical world offered new ways of organising with and against rulers and states. Even before the advent of the demos, the resolution to stand against power is embodied in the human frame of Achilles and Antigone. But Ionia also raises something even more decisive — that rests upon the fluidity and malleability of humans themselves. As humans design buildings, make sculptures, attach wings they also change themselves, not through compulsion, but through self-alteration. As Castoriadis notes of his own project:

> 'What is it that you want, then? To change humanity?'
> 'No, something infinitely more modest: simply that humanity change, as it has already done two or three times.'[18]

The Ionian spaces offer us autonomy, self-definition, extension, and self-determination. Ionia does not just construct automata that are fleeing from their masters and creators, but autonomous minds and bodies in a cycle of creation and re-creation.

Understanding the strata of human life and the bodies strewn across those strata means understanding our human entity as a confederation of archaic and newly emerging beings, coalitions and alliances of souls and phantasms coalescing in ever more complex variation. If Daedalus evaded his submergence into

---

18 Castoriadis, *Philosophy, Politics, Autonomy*, 275.

another being, a hybrid of human and bird, by using wings simply as tools, then we may not be so fortunate in our machines today, machines which have become part of our central being rather than prosthetic extensions to replicate animals and their capacities.

The Daedalian automaton is often perceived as a toy or a musical instrument, and is linked to the transmigration of the soul of the murdered Talos into a partridge (itself linked to the partridge dance of the maze). A second Talos emerges as the bronze automaton with a single vein stopped by a bronze pin which Medea unlocks to kill the monster.[19] The Greek αὐτόματον is often driven, in its mechanical being, by wind or blood—a combination of nature and technique. These archaic and elemental automata, what we might call ludic proto-robots, often have their will programmed within them but placed there by their maker.[20] In myth they become the playthings of children or the defenders of realms, ideas that are sustained into the medieval period, specifically the 'turning castle' of the Arthurian romances.

The ludic and musical aspects of the classical automata are also sustained into other civilisations—specifically the extant work of the Banu Musa and their ingenious devices in Islam and into the robots of the medieval period.[21] In fact the automata

---

[19] Robert Graves, *The Greek Myths (Combined Edition)* (Harmondsworth: Penguin, 1992), 311–15.

[20] Teun Koetsier, 'On the Prehistory of Programmable Machines: Musical Automata, Looms, Calculators', *Mechanism and Machine Theory* 36 (2001): 589–603.

[21] See David E. Creese, *The Monochord in Ancient Greek Harmonic Science* (Cambridge: Cambridge University Press, 2010), 51–53, where Creese examines the problematic relationship between musical instruments and the idea of scientific instruments—an idea that emerges only in early

are ubiquitous in classical sources as both monsters and playthings.[22] The most significant recent scholarly work by Francesca Berlinzari has examined the classical automaton as acoustic instrument, whether real or fictitious, and its ludic aspects and re-combinations.[23] There is some dissonance in classical accounts about whether the automata are made or whether they were born as descendants of the age of iron. Virgil's legend of the Iron Man and Talos the Bronze monster could have been either made or born. Perhaps the earliest extant account in the *Iliad* supports the idea that machines were the semblances of women, 'moving beneath their lord', and doing his bidding but sentient all the same. As J. Douglas Bruce notes in his discussion of those early accounts and in medieval manuscripts, there was probably little connection between these stories. He does, however, point out that in later discussions of the Daedalus myth there is a hint that his created automata were not machines but humans, and ones that rebelled against him and fled from him.[24]

The question of mechanics and materialism in the classical world has often rested upon understanding mechanistic modes of thought and their origin — something made even more

---

modernity. See also E.R. Truitt, *Medieval Robots: Mechanism, Magic, Nature, and Art* (Philadelphia: University of Pennsylvania Press, 2015).

22 Robert Sherrick Brumbaugh, *Ancient Greek Gadgets and Machines* (New York: Crowell, 1966) and Aage Gerhardt Drachmann, *The Mechanical Technology of Greek and Roman Antiquity: A Study of the Literary Sources* (Copenhagen: Munksgaard, 1963).

23 Francesca Berlinzani, 'Game, Ingenuity, Utopia. Acoustic Automata in the Greek and Roman World: Some Reflections/Gioco ingegno utopia. Automata sonori nel mondo *greco-romano*: Alcuni spunti di riflessione', *Lanx* 13 (2013): 27–51.

24 J. Douglas Bruce, 'Human Automata in Classical Tradition and Mediaeval Romance', *Modern Philology* 10, no. 4 (1913): 511–26.

problematic by the discovery of the Antikythera mechanism.[25] Sylvia Berryman has examined the origin of mechanical and teleological conceptions of humans and their world. Looking at mechanics may have influenced the ways in which the Greeks may have understood themselves as some sort of machine. Although her work stresses that mechanical conceptions were rooted in actual mechanics rather than the stories about previously existing automata the creation of 'life-like artifacts' often seemed like 'an imaginative precursor to the idea that organisms are like mechanical devices'.[26] As Berryman notes, however –'The relevant comparisons between natural and mechanical devices are not to artifacts that look like natural things, but those involving devices that could serve as a guide in investigating organic functions: they must be thought to work like them.'[27] The analogies between the mechanic and the organic would continue to be part of the continuing development of philosophy beyond the classical period.

The extension of the human into its minions, the ludic and acoustic proto-robots, was about will and where it resided. Even if the origin of the will was created by and still subordinate to the maker, defining automata was based on the will residing within the automaton itself (even if placed there) as an independent sentient being. These were not clockwork toys. Further, the danger posed by the minions and archaic machines of Daedalus lay in their becoming both rebellious

---

25 A.G. Bromley, 'Notes on the Antikythera Mechanism', *Centaurus* 29 (1986): 5–27.

26 Sylvia Berryman, 'Ancient Automata and Mechanical Explanation', *Phronesis: A Journal for Ancient Philosophy* 48, no. 4 (2003): 344–69, 345. See also Sylvia Berryman, *The Mechanical Hypothesis in Ancient Greek Natural Philosophy* (Cambridge: Cambridge University Press, 2009).

27 Berryman, 'Ancient Automata', 345.

and self-replicating. Certainly we see in the case of Talos that these machines could be machines of destruction, sometimes having the possibility not just of replication, but of redesigning themselves. They were new sentient and semantic machines — hybrid, mechanical, syncretic monsters. In their existential and physical threat to humans (and witness Medea destroying Talos by unpinning his vein) they begin to have the capacity, these monsters of their own invention, to submerge the mastery and identity of their masters. If the automaton is an extension of the human, then the automaton can turn back to that human and colonise it in turn.

Robert Sherrick Brumbaugh's eccentric and playful intervention into the ludics of the classical world is one of the few studies to take the classical machine seriously in its reconstruction of toys, automata, and tools. Brumbaugh hints that the compulsion to create machines is a product of an essential unity between the human nature of the classical past and of the contemporary world. The classical world created a 'capital of ideas' that remains with us.[28] The mechanical construction, specifically, of automata was about creating new beings with 'souls' as extensions of human beings:

> The designers of automata seem to have become progressively more ambitious, and their work more admired. Finally, by about the second century B.C. they aspired to nothing less than duplicating the most creative forms of human behavior with their self-propelled series of mechanical components. This idea of duplicating the powers of life by mechanisms must have reinforced the

---

28 Brumbaugh, *Ancient Greek Gadgets*, x.

highly speculative thesis of the atomic theory that all existing things are complex mechanisms...[29]

The idea that working with machines may have given classical humanity the idea that living beings were also machines further spurred the construction of new automata as human products. The multiple machines found at Knossos (a stamping machine, a pitcher, a three-dimensional map, gameboards, novelty libation jars), for Brumbaugh, confirmed the legend of the Daedalian myths — that '...certainly Daedalus had done *something* remarkable'.[30] Understanding the still extant Daidala sculptures as somehow the product of a real or legendary Daedalus would perhaps be of concern to recent scholarship, but they remain significant as an illustration of the imaginary power of craft and design. The Daidala sculptures could have their origins and significance in folklore and magic, represented artistic innovations, or even new mechanical innovations based around specific inventions. For Brumbaugh,

> The wonderful statues attributed to Daedalus come from, and refer back to, a period halfway between the world of science and mechanics and its precursor, a world of magic. The truth about these statues, which 'had to be kept chained, or they would run away,' has been a real challenge to scholarly ingenuity. In addition to their propensity to run away, there was something remarkable about the eyes of the statues: either they moved or in some other way gave the impression that they could actually see. Unlike the general inventions

---

29 Brumbaugh, *Ancient Greek Gadgets*, 5.
30 Brumbaugh, *Ancient Greek Gadgets*, 25.

the Minoans and Myceneans attributed to Daedalus, the story of the statues suggests some specific and remarkable innovations.[31]

For Brumbaugh the confusion about the automata lay not in thinking of machines as analogous with or copies of live human beings but a more classically oriented question — whether machines themselves were alive.[32] Certainly the fleeing automata display something distinctive about these specific Daedalian artefacts — that they were independent beings with their own will and not one imposed upon them or compelled to be within them by their maker.

There is also the significant question of the Daidalos diagrams referred to by Plato and what they signify for Platonist and Neo-Platonist philosophical practice as Plato reads them.[33] John Senseney's translation of Marsiglio Ficino's Neo-platonic commentary on the *Symposium* draws the links between the visualisation and philosophy:

> From the first moment the Architect conceives the reason and roughly the Idea of the building in his soul. Next he makes the house (as best he can) in such a way as it is available in his mind. Who will negate that the house is a body? And that this is very much like the incorporeal Idea of the craftsman, in whose imitation it has been

---

31 Brumbaugh, *Ancient Greek Gadgets*, 25–26.
32 Brumbaugh, *Ancient Greek Gadgets*, 58.
33 John R. Senseney, *The Art of Building in the Classical World: Vision, Craftsmanship, and Linear Perpective in Greek and Roman Architecture* (Cambridge: Cambridge University Press, 2011), 58–59.

made? Certainly it is more for a certain incorporeal order rather than for its material that it is to be judged.[34]

Senseney notes the relationship between the idea of the diagram and the models of machines as potentially part of the production of machines and mechanisms in the classical. He stresses the importance of the mechanisms of the Daidalos machine; 'The diagrams of Daidalos do not represent machines, but one's recognition of the element of *mechanism* that they relate to is important for understanding the world of made objects that Plato knew, as well as the transcendent truth of the universe that he describes'.[35] The incorporeal order made corporeal by craft and design hints at the emergence of imagination as a productive force — what Marx calls the machine as the organ and product of the human brain made material. But also the brain as a machine in itself.

As machines are assemblages in and of themselves of multiple components, so social forms are made of multitudes of machines and beings. These can range from specific automata toys, to war machines, buildings, the social machines of the digital world and abstract social machines which are almost undefinable and ineffable. For Gerald Raunig in his meditation on culture and machines,

> Is it about a machine? The question is not easy to answer, but correctly posed. The question should certainly not be: What is a machine? Or even: Who is a machine? It is not a question of the essence, but of the event, not about is, but about and, about concatenations and

---

34 Senseney, *Art of Building*, 9–10.
35 Senseney, *Art of Building*, 187.

connections, compositions and movements that constitute a machine.³⁶

His discussion of the origin of the classical machines hints at this decentred concept of the automaton.³⁷ But it also points to the whole social formation as a set of machines, fluid but territorially expansive. For Raunig,

> Abstract machines are things like this, which themselves have no form, are formless, amorphous, unformed. Yet their unformed-ness is not to be understood here as a lack, but rather as the ambivalent precondition for the emergence of fear as well as for the invention of new, terrifying forms of concatenation.³⁸

If our classical machines are connections and concatenations, compositions and movements what terrifying forms of concatenation might those machines emerge into? How will they self-alter and self-create as they are fleeing from their master and the essence that he imposed within and compelled within their being? In other words, how can the units of one assemblage resist the social powers of larger assemblages of forces, of creation and design but also subjection and violence. The labyrinth was the work of a human being, but that very human being was both murderer and tyrant, even as he himself was fleeing from the abstract and specific forces that threatened him with

---

36 Gerald Raunig, *A Thousand Machines: A Concise Philosophy of the Machine as Social Movement*, trans. Aileen Derieg (Los Angeles: Semiotext(e), 2010), 19.
37 Raunig, *Thousand Machines*, 37–39.
38 Raunig, *Thousand Machines*, 117.

imprisonment in his own labyrinth. When the automata created by human beings enslave human beings themselves, we find the productive forces becoming the forces of both reproduction and submission. For Marx,

> the means of labour passes through different metamorphoses, whose culmination is the *machine*, or rather, an *automatic system of machinery* (system of machinery: the *automatic* one is merely its most complete, most adequate form, and alone transforms machinery into a system), set in motion by an automaton, a moving power that moves itself; this automaton consisting of numerous mechanical and intellectual organs, so that the workers themselves are cast merely as its conscious linkages.[39]

The workers are neither the soul or the ghost of the system placed there by the makers of the automaton, nor can they flee, they are merely sentient appendages of the machine itself. The subjection to the machine is itself not a property of technique and automation but of the contingency and serendipity of the social relations surrounding the machine and compelling its advance.[40]

The role of the human, for Marx, is not to use the machine to produce and 'transmit the worker's activity to the object', but to aid the transmission of the action and work of the machine to the materials with which it is working.[41] The machine is the

---

39 Karl Marx, 'Fragment on Machines', in *Grundrisse: Foundations of the Critique of Political Economy (Rough Draft)*, trans. Martin Nicolaus (Harmondsworth: Penguin, 1973), 692.
40 Donald MacKenzie, 'Marx and the Machine', *Technology and Culture* 25, no. 3 (1984): 473–502, 500.
41 Marx, 'Fragment', 692.

engine of virtuosity, with its own mechanical soul and laws with the machine as part of the action of the automaton.[42] What begins with walking toys ends with machine domination.

The extension of the human in the classical world was then organic and combinatory as in the Centaurs, mechanical as in the automata, and architectural as in the Labyrinth. Each of these posed a danger in the destruction and mastery of the human maker in itself, but essentially they were extensions of the body in space; into minion proto-robots, into the being of other animals, into palaces. They were experiments in spatial extension, but they were also the beginning of the human compulsion to immortality — the extension of human beings in time, extending both territory and conquering history. This often meant becoming gods, or entering the realm of shades to continue their existence. At other times it meant metamorphosis into another being to sustain oneself or seeking sanctuary as a being in the body or soul of another and residing with them. The semantic machines of the classical world were replications of live things but also the template for new ways of understanding human beings themselves. The automata, the Centaurs, the monster at the heart of the labyrinth achieved the extension of their mechanisms and organisms into the cultures of future peoples, societies who would remain obsessed by these motifs whether they were used to ask the same questions asked by the classical world or had new uses in the social formations in which they were excavated and resurrected.

---

42 Marx, 'Fragment', 693.

chapter five

Ghosts, reading, and repetition

We have examined the *hybris* of Centaurs and the *hubris* of building labyrinths; the birth of organic beings and mechanical machines. The fleeing toys of Daedalus are part of the Never lands of the classical world as our abstract social machines gain more technical mastery over organic beings. Machines and organisms proliferate, concatenate, coalesce. New alliances and coalitions of forces emerge and disappear. The world determines. Beings self-determine. Social formations, epochs and civilisations alter human beings, human beings self-alter, extend, create proxy forces of minions and robots. Machines create proxy forces of human beings in contestations of data, of capital, of war. But human beings themselves also create the grounds for their own institution and transformation, new peoples coalesce and proliferate in new forms of genesis and regard, new formations are born out of different ways of thinking and living together, the new monstrous forces of impurity.

The striation and strata that we found embodied in the human mind and human culture from which art, craft, design, creation come and from which magical beings are excavated, recomposed, made to walk again, is clearly a geological analogy. Critically, these analogies have newly emerged to help understand the civilisational, epochal and geological moment in which we find ourselves. As an attempt to understand how to orient ourselves in this moment new theories of human design and intervention have recently emerged as new ways of theorising our worlds. There are contesting manners of measurement, of classification, and of periodization of the Anthropocene but it marks that historical and natural moment where human intervention in the world indelibly marks that world, changes its course, and stamps itself upon the geological strata of the earth.

Ionia is at least one of the moments where that indelible marking on the earth begins. The idea of the Anthropocene is situated in the emergence of the human as a being, a way that a species understands itself and its relation to inanimates and animates. The human itself becomes the animateur of non-sentient things, it manages, we might say, the 'dissentience' of its fleeing minions and machines. These are machines of extension, of domination, and subjection. Eventually they might come, as Marx says, to dominate their very makers but they are certainly interventions into nature. Devices to map cosmologies, like the Antikythera mechanism, were not there simply for curiosity and to display virtuosities of design but to aid the domination of nature through accumulation of knowledges and objects across seas. The idea of the power of these astrological repetitions have been admirably addressed by Keith Thomas, in his important work on religion and magic. It is particularly interesting in the sense that astrology is at the radical interface between a naturally occurring process (the movements of the planets) and its reception and impact on human processes and identity (believing that these planetary processes shape human history). The repetitions of the planetary processes are themselves repeated in the actions of all humanity, denoting a notion of the human being as compelled to repeat. Thomas notes that a purely astrological conception of fate was problematic in its rigidity — although in the scientific revolutions new planets were being discovered the limitation on the number of planets available to shape our destinies were few. This led to the fixing of human beings into a limited and vulgar typological system where the capacity for any degree of autonomy from the astrological repetitions was extremely limited. This idea of the radical restriction of human potentiality is an extremely important signifier of the perceived limitation of myth, motifs and personalities in the self-comprehensions of our era.[1]

The automata are engines of extension of the human social powers but they are also engines of extraction and accumulation — servile beings of warfare or household objects of their makers, doing their bidding. Like other human creations and gods these robots are like the *Lares* and *Penates* of the Roman household — household gods which protect, keep vigil and essentially serve still the people who live there.

One must not forget that the Centauromachy was a vision which elucidated the human relationship to other beings in the very hybridity of the human and the equine and as such was part of a process in which humans understood themselves qua other entities. But this was all the better to aid domination. The Centauromachy is not just a visual representation of different but entwined beings but one of war, genocide and destruction. The Lapiths and the Centaurs are locked in a deadly contest in Thessaly and one which will end with the banishment and eventual extinction of the Centaurs. The Centaurs were literally hunted out of the world, tracked down and destroyed, they are not

---

1   Keith Thomas, *Religion and the Decline of Magic: Studies in Popular Beliefs in Sixteenth and Seventeenth-century England* (Harmondsworth: Penguin, 1971), 385.

even visible in geological strata or excavation. Their fragments dispersed, their very material being extinguished. And why? Because they were barbaric, wilful, misbehaving, drunken, lascivious — they were not civilised. They were not part of the design of the new Anthropocene universe. The reversion to them in art and display would be a memorial not just to their absence but to their ethnic cleansing.

The Labyrinths, built as they were by humans, were part of the extension of human governance over nature. But they remained mysterious. The multicursal labyrinth of Minos, perhaps based on the Gortyna caves, was a place in which one could become lost. It was the thread of the soon-to-be-betrayed Ariadne which would guide Theseus to the centre. In trying to end the supremacy of Minos over tributary Athens Theseus sets himself the task of rescuing the tribute Athenian victims from the labyrinth. In order to do so he must also murder the hybrid Minotaur. The killing of the Minotaur marks then both the emergence of singular human and specifically Athenian domination over the Aegean cultures. The ritual re-enactment of the path through the maze to the centre was only made possible by the emergence of multiple, repetitive mazes but ones marked by an absence — that we have only the repetitions and echoes and not the original maze structure. Much like the Centaur, the original 'version' has gone or has never existed. The copies refract memories time and time again of their earlier versions but the 'Ur-motif' has disappeared, only its proliferations remain.

The return of archaic motifs are not just about absence but about abstraction and compression, about both extension and limitation. Abstraction is the extraction of something from its origin to a wider totality of time and history. The archaic structures and beings of classical Ionia are abstracted from their very specific origins in space and time, from a cave on Crete, or a valley in Thessaly, 3000 years ago into phantasms and Ur-motifs for global human cultures, becoming part of the imaginary capital of myth and matrices for their multiple versions and elaborations. The process of abstraction strips the entity of its locality, its vernacular, its mundanity, its provinciality whilst retaining, as clues, features that display its original existences and meanings at the same time as dispelling the idea of the 'authentic', which is itself inaccessible. The re-materialisation of the archaic entity time and time again in different historical and geographical conjunctures, often for wildly different reasons, is a re-production as much as it is a de-localisation. It's summoning up elevates aspects of the original, preserving some properties, but banishing other qualities. It has been extracted from the concrete and the specific into the geological, epochal, civilisational. This process of extra-territorialisation is literally one in which the 'dead seize the living'. Further, the use of these entities in those vastly different social, historical, geographical, geological locations hints again at the serendipitous and contingent emergence of their specific purpose in their moment of re-use. They are contingent not eternal identities depending on the specific social-historical imaginary which summons them again into being.

But these very processes of abstraction also display processes of compression, of time, of space, of the social world. These entities, structures, stories mean something to us not because they are distant but because of their 'nearness'. They have a proximity to us. This was all the more understandable in the context of the literality of biblical history of the earth as created and only four thousand years old. Genesis and Noah are in a sense proximal to us. They also have a proximity if those prophets, gods and angels are speaking in our ears in the here and now. If abstraction is about the relocation of specific entities and moments into the universal, civilisational, epochal, compression collapses those classifications and measurements making entities very close to us. In a sense that closeness becomes often a transmigration of souls as it were, as the beings and motifs of the 'dead generations' seize and inhabit our human frames as if they were refugees seeking for a place of safety, or to become active agents again having wandered around the world without corporeality.

The resurrections of the corporeal forms of classical Ionia are essentially, to use a term from classics, 'epigonic'. The heroes of the *Seven Against Thebes* produced multiple replications, literally the epigones — copies of those gone before.[2] Humans wanted to replicate stories of sacrifice and heroism, magnifying their own human frames and aspirations by compressing the distance between them and the ghosts they wanted to conjure up. This process of historical necromancy is at once recursive and repetitive, using the same old motifs that should have died with Athens but also profoundly creative as humans self-create, self-alter, self-elaborate, often with limited cultural means at their disposal. Why invent when we can repeat? But this might also be because of an ironic gesture inscribed in the heart of humanity — that the question about the instability of the human is actually part of the stability of a generalised and

---

2 It has its origins in the legend of The Seven Against Thebes — a fabled expedition by the seven Argive chiefs against the city of Thebes in Boeotia. All except one died. To avenge their deaths their seven sons undertook a new expedition, were successful and claimed the Theban crown. *Epigoni* literally means 'descendants' but is often used as a negative term to denote lesser descendants or followers.

continuing human nature that is born in our early civilisational moments. The reason that both abstraction and compression work for us is that they serve to answer the same questions, with the same motifs, stories and cultural resources, that were asked of and by humanity in its archaic birth as a self-defining and knowing species. It might literally be true that the reason we find the classical stories of incest and murder so compelling is that we struggle with the same problems as a human species.

The Centauromachy and its genocides, the murder of hybrid beings in labyrinths, the fall of the winged and engineered Icarus to his death display the victory of one type of anthropocentric, even Eurocentric, humanity. The relegation or destruction of the barbarians, the Persians, the monsters, the impure is part of a purification process in the heart of human beings. The pristine, exclusionary, solidification of one version of humanness will define future humanities. The fact that they summon up the monsters time and time again is a sublimation of their fears, horrors, dreams of others and themselves. It is almost as if they memorialise the beings and civilisations that they have exterminated and which only survive as fractured remnants into new epochs, cultures and locations.

The emergence of the human and the 'Achaean' is at the same time the birth of the idea of 'Europa' — the moment in which the Greeks triumph over the non-Greeks or barbarians. Whatever the ultimate origins of the Achaeans the birth of the idea of Europe is born in the struggles against the Persians and Greek expeditions into the hinterlands of Asia Minor. At the same time the exact location of 'Barbary' is opaque. In many ways it is 'Barbary' which maintains and sustains the fractured remnants of classical civilisation. The very idea of classical civilisation comes to be bound up with the 'Ionian spaces' of the temple, the demos, of law, justice and rationality and ultimately with technique. In this it stands not just against the Persians but also against the emergent monotheistic desert cults of Judaism, Christianity and Islam each of which in their own ways would become enmeshed with the classical.

The perpetual repetition of classical motifs would particularly come to fruition in the ideas of the English as Athenian or Trojan. Mythological histories tracing the early British kings from the Trojan diaspora would be formulated in the early medieval period. We also have the emergence, as we have seen, of the English towns of Troy and its labyrinths. Pseudo-historians have developed the idea of an English or Atlantic 'classical' world which displaces the Ionian locations of Odysseus with provincial English resorts, creating new maps of wanderings in different seas from those we had thought were the locations of the island of Circe. All of this is often a consequence of unauthorised and unmitigated *reading* in which we place Antigone into our own Never lands and locations and beings. This is reading in and *against* the classics. Rather than reading a text to know the world of its origin, or reading that world in order to know the text we come to read both text and world as the matrices of our own locations and imaginaries. We summon up the dead into our worlds rather than a reading which returns us into theirs. These dead suffer not one but many deaths, like the two deaths of Odysseus as he enters Hades and returns to the living to presumably return one day again to the underworld.

The Never lands do not just offer us Centaurs, labyrinths, automata—they offer us magic islands and underworlds, witches and gods, myths of genesis and metamorphosis. Later versions of antiquity would ultimately offer us political forms, science and philosophical practice. They would offer us slavery, incest and genocide and ways of challenging each. The dead remain with us as do the initial definitions of the human offered to us by the archaic classical world. The maps of that world display its instability and permeability — Scythians, Hyperboreans, Celts and beyond — the Argippaei, Issedones, Massagetae and the multiple lands of the Persian empire. Those peoples and empires have dissipated. Their ghosts remain — revenants who return into the present as corporeal or intangible beings. It is almost as if they are fleeing ghosts, shadows that have lost their bodies seeking refuge in new human frames. The materiality of their bodies have been extinguished but this does not mean finitude — they are recomposed and re-elaborated into new physical and emotional ensembles within human beings, incorporated. For many, as Castoriadis has noted, these were real, actual empirical beings that take possession of a child, or the divine manifestation once again in human form. These refuges hold real, transmigrated souls — the body becomes the new incarnation of a previous entity. Even trees or stones become the inhabitations of revenants. But there also the conjuring of pretense, of ghosts who are amalgams and exemplars of something else. Rather than a direct and empirical habitation of a human being the pretense and artifice of repetition acts as a form of *coding*, of speaking of something when it is difficult to do so in the terms of the present.

Margaret Rose, in her perceptive analysis of Marx's juvenilia, has examined the relationship between the ancients and the moderns in Marx, perceiving this relationship to be, at least partly, a response to coding and self-censorship in its widest possible sense:

> In Marx's poetry, this balance was often between the exoteric and the esoteric imagery of the text — where the ancient image (as Prometheus or Icarus in Marx's 1837 poems) would serve to express the essence of the modern situation which could not — for aesthetic or political reasons — be spoken of directly. Marx's use of the figures of Prometheus and Icarus as personae in his poems of 1836–7 both distances himself from the words of the text and points to this ambivalence in his work, in which contemporary and personal messages are masked by fictions borrowed from ancient or classical authors. The frequent use of parenthesis in Marx's poetry is an indication of the fear of direct expression and a means of saying things which otherwise — for personal or broader social reasons — had to be kept silent.[3]

These ghosts, like the body and the motif of Icarus, are literally fabricated and fictive beings re-assembled from the detritus of the past. They are also often pathological repetitions. The world is not conjured up out of nothing but out of the resources to hand, literally an index in which one can look up the ghosts which one would like to use. Embodiment itself then becomes a coding process in which the repetition of faces, forms, appearances — the surface — displays the haunting, but without the haunting and the ghost within. As Bhabha has said — 'It is the problem of how, in signifying the present, something comes to be repeated, relocated and translated in the name of tradition, in the guise of a pastness that is not necessarily a faithful sign of

---

3 Margaret A. Rose, *Reading the Young Marx and Engels: Poetry, Parody and the Censor* (London: Croom Helm, 1978), 36–37.

historical memory but a strategy of representing authority in terms of the artifice of the archaic'.[4] The artifice of the archaic is relocation, re-embodiment, but one which is still part of the extension and the re-elaboration of human possibilities and the incorporation of ghostly powers of authority in human form.

We can see the force of the processes of natural and social repetition and some initial clues to the supersession of this repetitive process in the work of Freud and his notion of the compulsion to repeat as both an instinctual and a learned, social process. The ubiquity of repetition is explained by Freud as a clear, if distorted, consequence of natural behaviours. In the *New introductory lectures on Psychoanalysis* Freud develops a key notion of repetition where the process of repetition inherent within nature degenerates into the fatalistic acceptance within the human psyche of repetitive (and overwhelmingly destructive behaviour).[5]

Firstly, Freud attaches great importance to a notion of instinctual force which constantly wishes to restore a previous state of being. Much like a conception of a return to Eden, the instincts govern all mental and biological life, and they constantly try to return the mind or the organism as a whole to a previous 'state of things' — an earlier moment which can only be resurrected if the instinctual force succeeds. Because each state has to be temporary in the flux of both evolution and history each of these states is condemned to be surpassed. The instinct then arises in order to compel the organism to return to that state. This 'compulsion to repeat' manifests itself in all organisms.

---

4   Homi K. Bhabha, *The Location of Culture* (London: Routledge, 1994), 35.
5   Sigmund Freud, *New Introductory Lectures on Psychoanalysis* (Harmondsworth: Penguin, 1973), 139–40.

Freud uses the example of embryology to illustrate the ways in which the instincts attempt to generate this repetitive process of the genesis of organisms. The capacity for the regeneration of lost organs is still present within some organisms in an attempt to restore the lost status of a full being. Freud himself notes the role of therapy as an attempt to recover a lost balance or state of being — an attempt at the repetition of innocence. The migrations of fishes and birds and the repetitive process observable within nature generally all testify to the power of attempts to return or resurrect the previous state of being. Crucially, for Freud, this compulsion is part and parcel of a reactionary or conservative instinctual process. The return, repetition or resurrection is an attempt not at liberation from the past evolutionary chain or historical process but an attempt to submerge the life of the present organism within the mass of the past.

Secondly, for Freud, it is clear that this compulsion is present within all human mental endeavour. It manifests itself particularly in the pathological and detrimental situation of those whose mental state condemns them to the perpetual repetition of various kinds of actions, behaviours, motifs. The compulsion to repeat destructive patterns here, not only reflects a conservative rather than liberative process but expresses to those repeating the actions the pressure of a 'relentless fate' brought upon them not by themselves but by other powers such as the instincts ruling the natural world, religious conceptions of destiny and so on. Freud's psychoanalytic investigations — the empirical observation and description of these processes — reveals to him, and the patient with the pathological disorder, that liberation of oneself from such compulsions entails the liberation from conceptions of an overwhelming fate. In other words the recognition that one's fate lies in one's own hands means the achievement of that very self-determining fate.[6]

One of the most important aspects of the recurrence of these residual and anachronistic forms that are not benign is that of the replication in different, yet perhaps similar, historical moments of an originary, archetypal historical figure, commonly an Alexander or a Caesar. This process had been recognised at the beginning of the modern period and conceptualized as a form of *prosopopoeia*; the conceptual form of personification (literally to make faces) which denotes the idea of a representation of an imaginary, absent or dead person speaking and acting. It is an absence which is made to be present, conjured up from the past and recomposed in the here and now. An interesting elaboration of these themes can be found in Foucault and his fellow researchers' recovery of the case of Pierre Rivière, where the crimes perpetrated by a young man upon his mother, his sister and his brother found their sanction in his conception of himself as the personal repetition of his dead heroes. The murderer's memoirs provide an insight into the nature of repetition and the recomposition of characters of example and instruction. They exemplify the ways in which the will of an individual incorporates and uses elements from wider structural lineages.

Pierre Rivière found his glory in being the epigone of preceding exemplary characters. The executor of the will of providence Rivière had, since childhood, fantasized about his heroes, imagining some form of identity with them, conjuring them

---

6 Freud, *Lectures*, 139–40.

up in his actions.⁷ His enemies were the cabbages in his garden arrayed as armies which, as a great general, he would destroy.⁸ This vivid imagination was largely the consequence of his idiosyncratic reading and his religious passion — torturing and sacrificing small animals to reproduce the scenes of Christ's passion.⁹ Consumed by a conception of himself as one of the great men he admired, he would achieve the dignity denied to him in his life: 'I made up stories in which I imagined myself playing a role, I was forever filling my head with personages I imagined'.¹⁰ This begins to take a more sinister turn as the relationship between his mother and his father deteriorates. This section of his confession is worth examining in more depth.

Rivière had read in his history books about ancient Rome that the laws of the period gave the man of the household the right of life and death over wife and family. Conceiving of himself, at this moment, as the bastion of Roman law against the French legal code, he conjures up this past to sustain himself in his sacrifice to uphold the rights of the father and the patriarchy against the mother and his siblings. The defiance of the contemporary laws and his immortalization in the eyes of the past then lead him to the identification of himself with those students who took up arms at the taking of Paris in 1814 giving their lives for a leader who they did not know and who did not know them. If they were willing to die for an abstraction indifferent to their fate then how fitting it would be for Rivière to sacrifice himself for the empirical, knowable father whom he loved and

---

7   Michel Foucault, *I, Pierre Rivière, Having Slaughtered My Mother, My Sister, and My Brother . . . A Case of Parricide in the 19th Century*, trans. Frank Jellinek (Harmondsworth: Penguin, 1978), 193.
8   Foucault, *Rivière*, 101.
9   Foucault, *Rivière*, 128.
10 Foucault, *Rivière*, 102–03.

who loved him in return. A series of exemplars pass through his consciousness — Chatillon dying in the streets to save his king, Eleazar the Maccabee slaying an elephant knowing he would die beneath its weight, a Roman general whose name Rivière forgets dying in the war against the Latins — 'All these things passed through my mind and invited me to do my deed'. The example of Henri de la Roquejacquelin becomes particularly appropriate. Dying to uphold the cause of the King, 'I pondered his harangue to his soldiers as the battle began: if I advance, he said, follow me, if I retreat kill me, if I die avenge me'. Even a book of shipwrecks and the sacrifices made by the sailors inspires him to seek the death of his mother. Finally we come to the example of Christ upon the cross. Redeeming humanity and forgiving them he could have punished the sinners and could have pardoned them without suffering crucifixion, 'but as for me, I can deliver my father only by dying for him'.[11] Rivière's is a master and slave dialectic, the downtrodden father deprived of the rights given to him by the past will have the current order overturned by his son who will reclaim what is his. It is interesting then that he uses female slaves to overturn order, power and dictatorship, perhaps because he considers these masters to be those who held power in the present social formation — a power which had been delegated to a mother rather than to the rightful upholder of the traditions of the past — 'Jaels against Siseras, Judiths against Holofernes, Charlotte Cordays against Marats'.[12] and perhaps most fittingly, in the aftermath of all the overturnings of the revolution, empire and restoration, he conjures up that ghost who seems to be everywhere at once, Napoleon Bonaparte.

---

11 Foucault, *Rivière*, 106.
12 Foucault, *Rivière*, 107–08.

The judicial commentaries on the case refer tellingly to Rivière as 'an unfinished being,'[13] the books he read providing the template and justification for the murder of his sister and mother. His memoir is full of contradictions and delusions but it also hints at the notion of completeness which could be conferred by the combination of his own consciousness with those of the past. Foucault and his fellow researchers, almost as an afterthought and without pursuing it to any depth, begin to think about this aspect of the memoirs by examining this copying of the 'illustrious models' he had collected from his idiosyncratic historical and theological reading. As a half-conscious repetition of exemplars such as Julian Sorel, Saint-Just and Don Quixote they note his resurrection and re-enactment of the obligations of ancient codes.[14] But the central part of this is the index of his reading:

> I had ideas of glory, I took great pleasure in reading. At school they read the Royaumont Bible, I read in Numbers and Deuteronomy, in the Gospel and the rest of the New Testament, I read in Almanacs and geography, I read in the Family Museum and a clergy calendar, some histories, that of Bonaparte, Roman history, a history of shipwrecks, the Practical Morals and several other things.[15]

And in the commentaries it is noted that the historical reading was the condition which made murder and morbidity possible as almost a form of memoir. Accumulating and having

---

13 Foucault, *Rivière*, 152.
14 Foucault, *Rivière*, 185.
15 Foucault, *Rivière*, 101–02.

knowledge becomes the index of both elaboration and murder.[16] For Rivière himself he becomes the exemplar and embodiment of the human possibilities of incorporating ghosts within one's person. The artifice of the archaic is extracted by reading from the sum of historical knowledge to date:

> I thought it would be a great glory to me to have thoughts opposed to all my judges, to dispute against the whole world, I conjured up Bonaparte in 1815. I also said to myself: that man sent thousands to their death to satisfy mere caprices, it is not right therefore that I should let a woman live who is disturbing my father's peace and happiness, I thought that an opportunity had come for me to raise myself, that my name would make some noise in the world, that by my death I should cover myself with glory, and that in time to come my ideas would be adopted and I would be vindicated.[17]

George Kubler was one of the first theorists to really delineate the impact of repetition in culture and art and the power of repetitious forms. Kubler makes an obvious key distinction between the primary invention and the series of replications of that invention. An original work of art becomes the template for an inexhaustible series of secondary imitations or mutations within a, particularly aesthetic, genre. This leads Kubler to meditate on the method of the structural limitation of the motif:

---

16 Foucault, *Rivière*, 209.
17 Foucault, *Rivière*, 108.

Human desires in every present instant are torn between the replica and the invention, between the desire to return to the known pattern, and the desire to escape it by a new variation. Generally the wish to repeat the past has prevailed over the impulses to depart from it. No act ever is completely novel, and no act can ever be quite accomplished without variation. In every act, fidelity to the model and departure from it are inextricably mingled, in proportions that ensure recognisable repetition, together with such minor variations as the moment and the circumstances allow.[18]

For Kubler these repetitions are not the product of will or human choice but are the highly-determined products of the object or phenomena's structural lineage. Abandoning any conception of human penetration into the binding system of what he calls 'replica-mass' Kubler 'over-structuralizes' the whole idea of instauration and repetition. For Kubler the situation of any 'creator' is rigidly determined by the lineages within which their work is situated. The previous sequences of events determine the replications which will ensue. At the same time this system is invisible to the creator and, unperceived, becomes a retarding force on their own creativity — limiting in its very invisibility. This invisible force structures certain kinds of circumstances within which the actions are predetermined. The consequence of this is the rigid acceptance of the structure or a rebellion against that structure to replace the original piece of art with something which is not a replication. What Kubler calls the 'congenital peculiarities of temperament' can react

---

18 George Kubler, *The Shape of Time: Remarks on the History of Things* (New Haven: Yale University Press, 1962), 72.

against the replica-mass but can only create an anti-order. This is not the negative of other parts of the replica-mass but a chaotic phenomenon without form, because it is without history.[19]

Each new form is imprisoned by previous forms and in turn acts as a constraint upon the development of subsequent forms.[20] The dialectic here is between a repetition in the human world which is exact and 'onerous' and a new variation which is 'unfettered' and chaotic. Neither of these, for Kubler, is a real possibility.[21] As Kubler makes clear in his limitation of his own argument, there is no true identity between objects, motifs, people — there can only be an imagined repetition and identity. Every event or phenomena does differ from what has come before it — identity is a fiction, each act an invention of sorts.

But, in a practical way we all seek the consolations and consolidations of accepted form. Unable to accept the infinitude of motifs we structure finite systems of motifs which come to bind us to certain courses of action in our art and our politics. If events are, in reality, non-repeatable we still understand history with a secondhand historical consciousness which can only make sense by constructing identities and analogies.[22] This is why we are constantly tuned to this 'epigonal tenor' — recursiveness is part of our ways of understanding the flux of history.

For Kubler the originary archetype of the object provides the template for a series of divergences accumulated in the dialectic between pure repetition or replication and invention. Backwards to what is known or forwards to pure invention or the instauration of new forms. In reality each action is a curious

---

19 Kubler, *Shape of Time*, 50.
20 Kubler, *Shape of Time*, 54.
21 Kubler, *Shape of Time*, 63.
22 Kubler, *Shape of Time*, 67.

tension between these compulsions—recognisable recurrences continue, minute variations adapt as the force of circumstance, the past might allow.[23] When Kubler begins to study the kinds of meanings which are attributed to or extracted from forms which are repeated we can see the overwhelming power of these amalgams. Individuals and communities recognise in cultural form shared symbolic notations. They can come to perceive meaning in something purely by dint of its repetition in current circumstances. It provides a kind of habitation for these shared meaning to express themselves.[24] This leads us then to a consideration not only of Kubler's structural determinants of repetition but the active shaping of meaning inherent in the inheritance and use of the anachronistic forms. The imagined power takes hold.

The residues of prior social formations are often vernacular, mundane resistances to dominant cultures.[25] An interesting example of such a residual form is Carlo Ginzburg's important research on the complex case of Menocchio and his peculiar theology gleaned from his idiosyncratic reading of past texts. This was transformed into something quite profound in a fascinating dialectic between the literate culture to which he partly had access to and the oral culture from which he had emerged:

> Thus a mass of composite elements, ancient and not so ancient, came together in a new construction. An almost unrecognisable fragment of a capital, or the half-obliterated outline of a pointed arch, might jut out from

---

23 Kubler, *Shape of Time*, 71–72.
24 Kubler, *Shape of Time*, 74.
25 Raymond Williams, *Problems in Materialism and Culture* (London: Verso, 1980), 40.

a wall: but the design of the edifice was his, Menocchio's. With an unselfconscious and open mind he made use of remnants of the thinking of others as he might stones or bricks. But the linguistic and conceptual tools that he tried to acquire were neither neutral nor innocent. This is the explanation for most of the contradictions, uncertainties, and incongruities of his speeches. Using terms infused with Christianity, neo-Platonism, and scholastic philosophy, Menocchio tried to express the elemental, instinctive materialism of generation after generation of peasants.[26]

Again, idiosyncratic reading does not just summon up isolated fragments but recomposes them into a new cosmological assemblage profoundly at odds with the cultures and social imaginaries of the ascending and dominant social forces.

To conceive of a different and more positive sense of repetition we can read, with Gillian Rose, Kierkegaard's point about nostalgia — that repetition and recollection are the same movement but in opposite directions.[27] John D. Caputo argues, in his own commentary on Kierkegaard, for this distinction between repetition and recollection — 'Repetition thus is not the repetition of the same, Greek re-production, but a creative production which pushes ahead, which produces as it repeats, which produces what it repeats, which makes a life for itself in the midst of the difficulties of the flux'.[28] Repetition is not

---

26 Carlo Ginzburg, *The Cheese and the Worms: The Cosmos of a Sixteenth-century Miller* (Harmondsworth: Penguin, 1992), 61.

27 Gillian Rose, *The Broken Middle: Out of Our Ancient Society* (Oxford: Basil Blackwell, 1992), 88.

28 John D. Caputo, *Radical Hermeneutics: Repetition, Deconstruction and the Hermeneutic Project* (Bloomington: Indiana University Press, 1987), 3.

copying but using mimicry to orient ourselves in our world, as mysterious to us as the classical world was to the Achaeans.

Similarly, in his analysis of fictional resemblance Joseph Hillis Miller notes that resemblances can be perceived in a similar way as we perceive a metaphor — a displacement of meaning away from the place where it had its origin. This transportation ensures the construction of analogies, perceived repetitions and similar forms but cannot be understand as 'pure' repetitions or identities in any way.[29] Hillis Miller's points are useful in our discussion here because they not only help us to understand the ubiquity of repetition in fiction but also because of the similarity between fictional and historical techniques of writing. The recomposition of real people, ideas and so on within historical writing relies on the same techniques of metaphor and analogy — even if the processes and people which inhabit history are objects of real, empirically definable existence whilst fictional ones rest within a very different epistemological territory. We can achieve some sense of this ubiquity of repetition in history by looking at some of the devices of repetition that Hillis Miller examines in fiction.

Hillis Miller argues that fictional characters can repeat processes visible in their ancestors or conjure up within themselves historical and mythological personalities. These lock into wider processes of repetition observable in the fiction — all repetitious processes observable inside the text. This can be achieved in the consciously chosen repetitious behaviour freely chosen (within structural constraints) by the protagonists or an objectively imposed understanding on behalf of the author — a perceived repetition of which the protagonist is unaware. The

---

29 Joseph Hillis Miller, *Fiction and Repetition: Seven English Novels* (Oxford: Basil Blackwell, 1982), 14.

dialectic between the original and the repetition is a complex one and one where the subjective and the objective and the individual and the historical interpenetrate. But the fiction can also repeat things external to the text — the author's mind or biography, the wider historical process and the motifs it creates, works by other writers and even events occurring (in the fictional world) before the book begins.[30] Even the most abstract, fantastic, work of fiction betrays its affinity to the world external to the text — it would make no sense to the reader if there weren't shared vocabularies, motifs and so on. A work of history is even more immersed in the world it is trying to represent. In obvious ways the historical work does make reference to the partisan who is writing the work but if there were no reference or congruence between the world and the text then it would not purport to be even a historical representation. Examples of the process by which historical writing in representing the real uses devices from fiction and mythology does not mean that such tools of telling stories lead to fictional renditions.

Following Deleuze, Hillis Miller also makes the distinction between two broad forms of repetition — what Deleuze calls 'Platonic' repetition and 'Nietzschean' repetition. The first is that repetition which tries to conform, to correspond to a 'solid archetypal model'.[31] The second form rests upon an idea of difference — that the world is not based upon copying but of the proliferation of 'phantasms' ungrounded in archetypal figures which urge forms of copying. These phantasms are not anchored in any meaningful way to that originary object, motif, or personality. It is a free-floating world of ghosts and resemblances rather than a vulgar reality of original and copy.

---

30 Miller, *Fiction and Repetition*, 2–3.
31 Miller, *Fiction and Repetition*, 6.

In other words, whilst one works with realities and the identities between them which can be examined and explained by recourse to a resolving of the phantom into the material historical process the other is much more opaque and mystificatory.

The fact that, as we have seen, the young Marx conjures up Prometheus and Icarus in his juvenilia is not itself a source of surprise. Reading the classics was by default part of a classical education — particularly in a period in which multiple moments of the classical past were resurrected in architecture, philosophy and politics. What perhaps is surprising is Marx's lifetime obsession with the camera obscura that witnesses ghosts. Marx is obsessed with a specific sense of social haunting as Derrida has noted in his own obsessive reading of the ghosts in Marx and specifically the *18 Brumaire*, itself a classical motif. As Derrida says — 'The Eighteenth Brumaire of Louis Bonaparte deploys once again, on the same frequency, something like a spectropolitics and a genealogy of ghosts . . . Marx never stops conjuring and exorcising there'.[32] In recent years there has been a resurgence of interest in Marx's *Eighteenth Brumaire* in traditions often noted for their hostility to any notion of historical materialism. Jacques Derrida speaks of the work, as we have already noted, as 'a genealogy of ghosts'[33] where the presence of the spectre in human form provides the basis for a new reading of a Marx obsessed with the notion of hauntings and reversion. Derrida's reading and explication of Marx reforms Marx's notion of the *remplacants* as forms of 'revenants' — spectres who find their expression in real human form — spirits which become corporeal through taking over

---

32 Jacques Derrida, *Specters of Marx: The State of the Debt, the Work of Mourning, & the New International*, trans. Peggy Kamuf (London: Routledge, 1994), 107.
33 Derrida, *Specters of Marx*, 107.

the bodies of human beings.[34] This conception of phantoms, inheritance and repetition becomes a way of consolidating a strategic, revolutionary perspective based upon the 'politics of memory'.[35] This concept of visitation is an important and complex one in Derrida's analysis. It signifies the sense that a spirit appears and begins to inhabit the present. It can be an apparition which is positive and can be welcomed but at the same time, for Derrida, 'it can signify strict inspection or violent search, consequent persecution, implacable *concatenation*. The social mode of haunting, its original style it could also be called, taking into account this repetition, *frequentation*'.[36] The visitation demands that it be able to enquire and inspect, bringing together the past and the future, actuality and imagination — the 'social mode' of the return implying a constancy of visitation, a frequentation of the inspecting ghost.

Yet, unable to and not wanting to negate Marx's constant adherence to a materialist form of explaining such phenomena, Derrida recognises that for Marx there was a very real distinction between the world of ghosts and that of materiality. Yet in reaffirming this Derrida then makes the claim that these supposedly weightless phenomena — spectres — could only weigh on the minds of the living and particularly on revolutionaries if they had some kind of 'spectral density'.[37] How, then, can these phenomena, having no existence external to the mind of the one comprehending their frequentation have such a material presence? For Derrida these 'implacable anachronies'[38] become

---

34 Derrida, *Specters of Marx*, 4.
35 Derrida, *Specters of Marx*, xix.
36 Derrida, *Specters of Marx*, 101.
37 Derrida, *Specters of Marx*, 109.
38 Derrida, *Specters of Marx*, 116.

weighted by becoming present in human form and human structures instituting forms of spirit which have real material consequences. Again we see the ways in which the conjuring up of the spirits of the dead become forces which can transform political and historical moments. Instituting the reign of death within life they cannot however propel us backwards to Never lands and lost paradises.

When Gillian Rose came to think about the presence of ancient societies, classical social forms, and Ionian thinking in the midst of our society she noted that the persistence of repetition marked a confusion about who we are and where we are going as a human species. It marked for her the absence and abandonment of the 'historical telos', the foregrounding of the body and corporeality, and the elision not just of thought and being, but also of metaphors about who we were.[39] Repetition and the necromancy of the dead beings and forms of the classical world mark not just questions of the stability or instability of the human as an entity but also something else. Reading, abstraction, the capacity to 'look up' in an index provides the forms and essence of who we are or want to become. The dead become refugees in our own human forms because of this very instability between on the one hand the 'entity that is', our being in the world, our corporeality and materiality in the world of life and on the other the capacity of our thought and imaginaries to be structured by and full of the detritus of the past. Our very cosmologies are new assemblages of the archaic and the novel, living and dead. We build our new Troys and wooden horses with Ionia and the Achaeans looking on as visitants within us.

---

39 Rose, *Broken Middle*, xiv.

conclusion

Centaurs, human and non-human

On the third of January 1889 the erstwhile classical philologist and philosopher Friedrich Nietzsche ran to a horse on the Piazza Carlo Alberto in Turin that was being whipped. Protecting and embracing the horse this episode signalled what would be the final break in his sanity. Beginning to describe himself as Dionysus, as a god walking amongst humans in a world in which he had already scented the divine decomposition, Nietzsche began his final descent into the realm of inwardness, ultimately surrendering any relation to the world beyond him.[1] The vision of this curious Turin Horse comprised of man and beast becoming Dionysus also hints at those ferocious followers of that god: the Maenads. Likened by Euripides to fillies or wild horses, the Maenad women tear humans apart like the monstrous horses of the classical world. One of the defining questions that Roberto Calasso has asked is about this sense of inwardness — 'What went on inside the Maenad?'[2]

Yet if humans can become gods in the metamorphosis between the human and equine, or in the heart of the labyrinth or in

---

1 Malek K. Khazaee, 'The Case of Nietzsche's Madness', *Existenz* 3, no. 1 (2008), https://existenz.us/volumes/Vol.3-1Khazaee.html.
2 Roberto Calasso, *The Marriage of Cadmus and Harmony*, trans. Tim Parks (New York: Alfred A. Knopf, 1993), 308.

the machines that they extend themselves with, it also means that the earth that was built by the gods for their 'raids, whims, intrigues, experiments'[3] is now surveyable by humans as the place of their own raids, whims, intrigues, experiments. If the humans can make gods, make themselves gods, even depose gods, the earth itself becomes their labyrinth, made by a man as Castoriadis is intent upon saying. This entails both the destruction and the perpetuation of the Olympian cosmology, but in the emergence and the proliferation of species and their merging, their *hubris*, we also see the emergence of the human social world, collectivities, and the capacity to survey it, bit by bit. The persistence of the classical detritus, its remnants and fragments, is still central to our self-understanding. That world is still with us, in our many forms of inwardness, but also in our self-institution of the world we now make around us.

Understanding the social weight of ghosts and phantasms, of Centaurs, Labyrinths, and Automata entails a description of their quantities, qualities, and properties as they re-emerge in new locations. Understanding the entity means demarcating between different properties and the caesura between them, a caesura that is both a border and a seam. The caesura is then at once a break or an interruption between elements but also a junction and a suture. There may be fractures, fissures, abysses between those elements but this is not a closure, or an irredeemable gap. The seam is both a wall and a conjuncture. Further, in a different sense the seam is also a line within strata, a layer which can be excavated or mined not just to understand the existence or non-existence of entities within those strata but also to examine the strata interior to being.

---

3 Calasso, *Marriage*, 89.

CONCLUSION: CENTAURS, HUMAN AND NON-HUMAN

For Giorgio Agamben the comprehensibility of the human is only made possible by understanding the borders and seams between the human and non-human, the properties they share and those they do not. This leads not to division and difference, but to the ultimate reconciliation between the animal and the human.[4] The question then lies in the metamorphosis of its individual parts, their separation and their proximity, into the ultimate and definitive annihilation of the human element or the destruction of the animal element.[5] Even before we reach that moment we still have, however, problems of defining the border, the caesura, between its components.[6] For Agamben, in his reflections on Kojève reading Hegel,

> man is not a biologically defined species, nor is he a substance given once and for all; he is, rather, a field of dialectical tensions always already cut by internal caesurae that every time separate — at least virtually — 'anthropophorous' animality and the humanity which takes bodily form in it. Man exists historically only in this tension; he can be human only to the degree that he transcends and transforms the anthropophorous animal which supports him, and only because, through the action of negation, he is capable of mastering and, eventually, destroying his own animality.[7]

---

4   Giorgio Agamben, *The Open: Man and Animal*, trans. Kevin Attell (Stanford: Stanford University Press, 2004), 3–6.
5   Agamben, *Open*, 10.
6   Agamben, *Open*, 59.
7   Agamben, *Open*, 12.

The coalescence of forces, entangled conglomerations of beings, make the question of the interior and inwardness as important as the external, visual properties of the entity. The human has mobile and metamorphosing borders within.[8] Humans are the locations for these metamorphoses and the result of what Agamben calls the 'ceaseless divisions and caesurae?'[9]

The idea of the caesura holds within biological entities but equally also for those beings which are hybrids of biology and mechanics — what Bernard Stiegler calls 'technical beings' as a 'complex of heterogenous forces'.[10] These entities are complexes of machine and organism but also of outwardness and inwardness, what Stiegler calls the exterior milieu of nature and the interior milieu of social memory, collective historical memory and culture.[11] The relations between the human and their external worlds resulted in the aspirational technical capacity of humans to augment themselves in a 'movement of planetary extension'.[12] But Stiegler also thinks deeply about the origins of these human beings in classical Greece and the accidental and necessary predicates of what being human means as a species.[13] If the human, for Steigler is invented, who or what invents that human?[14] For Stiegler — 'We are considering a passage: the passage to what is called the human. Its "birth," if there is one. Why should we question the "birth" of the human?

---

8   Agamben, *Open*, 15.
9   Agamben, *Open*, 16.
10 Bernard Stiegler, *Technics and Time, 1: The Fault of Epimetheus*, trans. Richard Beardsworth and George Collins (Stanford: Stanford University Press, 1998), 2.
11 Stiegler, *Technics*, 57.
12 Stiegler, *Technics*, 90.
13 Stiegler, *Technics*, 95–97.
14 Stiegler, *Technics*, 134.

CONCLUSION: CENTAURS, HUMAN AND NON-HUMAN

First of all because we have unceasingly, since Hegel, questioned its end'.[15]

The reflexive self-making and alteration of humans is the very designation and definition of the human — it only becomes human through 'technics' and the mastery of nature at the same time as technics becomes the master of human beings as themselves part of nature.[16] The dialectic between the physical and the biological creates the grounds for the emergence of the technical object — the organized and distributed 'inorganic being' which is itself not simply material or animal but the product of both.[17] As Stiegler says,

> The problem arising here is that the evolution of this essentially technical being that the human is exceeds the biological, although this dimension is an essential part of the technical phenomenon itself, something like its enigma. The evolution of the "prosthesis," not itself living, by which the human is nonetheless defined as a living being, constitutes the reality of the human's evolution, as if, with it, the history of life were to continue by means other than life: this is the paradox of a living being characterized in its forms of life by the nonliving — or by the traces that its life leaves in the nonliving.[18]

The question of the origins of the human as Stiegler notes is therefore a question of its end. This means not just the mechanical and biological seams and borders within entities, but the

---

15 Stiegler, *Technics*, 135.
16 Stiegler, *Technics*, 24.
17 Stiegler, *Technics*, 26.
18 Stiegler, *Technics*, 50.

properties of the living and the non-living in beings, the mesh of and the permeability between the animal and the human. As we build our biological (if mythical) beings like Centaurs, as we engineer our technical objects like labyrinths, as we create purely non-sentient machines like automata, as we augment and combine biology and machine, we are at both the birth and the extinction of humanity. If the *making* animal of the classical world has to come to an end, it will engineer its extinction itself in its very act of humanness. The properties of the animal or of the machine that are present within those human complexes of interiority and exteriority may subsume its human components, albeit in different ways.

The Centaurs, even if they emerged from the Thessalian darkness, did not emerge without ancestries, lineages, continuities, and monstrous couplings. If they are invented just as much as the human, then we have to ask who or what made them and who or what made the Maenads, the gods, the Furies. But in describing that birth we also describe their own ends and endings and map their own lineages and continuities and couplings into our own worlds; enduring, creating, metamorphosing.

www.ingramcontent.com/pod-product-compliance
Lightning Source LLC
Chambersburg PA
CBHW070848160426
43192CB00012B/2350